CULTURAL REVOLUTION, CULTURE WAR:

HOW CONSERVATIVES LOST ENGLAND AND HOW TO GET IT BACK

BY SEAN GABB

GW00499469

I give not Heav'n for lost. From this descent
Celestial vertues rising, will appear
More glorious and more dread than from no fall,
And trust themselves to fear no second fate....
(Milton, PL ii, 14-17)

The Hampden Press
London
2007

Cultural Revolution, Culture War: How Conservatives Lost England, and How to Get It Back, by Sean Gabb

© The Hampden Press, Sean Gabb, 2007

This first edition published in August 2007

The right of Sean Gabb to be identified as the author of this work has been asserted hereby in accordance with the Copyright, Designs and Patents Act 1988.

Published by
The Hampden Press
Suite 35
2 Landsdowne Row
London W1J 6HL
England

Telephone: 07956 472 199
E-mail: *directors@hampdenpress.co.uk*
Web: *www.hampdenpress.co.uk*
Directors: Dr Sean Gabb, Mario Huet

ISBN: 0-9541032-2-X
ISBN 13/EAN 9780954103224

British Library Cataloguing in Publication Data: A catalogue record for this book is available from the British Library

Printed and bound by Biddles Ltd, 24 Rollesby Road, Hardwick Industrial Estate, King's Lynn, Norfolk, PE30 4LS

Registered in England and Wales No.00158041

I DEDICATE THIS BOOK
TO ALL THOSE MANY
WHO CONTRIBUTED TO THE COST OF
PUBLISHING IT;

AND TO THE MEMORY OF CHRISTOPHER
RONALD TAME (1949-2006),
MY LEADER, MY COLLEAGUE, MY FRIEND;

AND TO MY DEAR WIFE, ANDREA, WITHOUT
WHOSE PATIENCE
AND UNDERSTANDING
I MIGHT NEVER
HAVE WRITTEN A WORD

CONTENTS

FRONT COVER: *Death or Liberty!* by George Cruickshank, December 1818
(detail)

INTRODUCTION: ENGLAND, JULY 2007

Those who wish to change the world must first understand it. Unless we can know where we are, and why, we cannot hope to end where we want to be. And for those traditionalist Tories, classical liberals and libertarians who comprise the British conservative movement, the first step to understanding is to accept that we have lost the battle for this country.

The Blair Government was not an aberration from an otherwise healthy state of affairs. Its social and political acts were not "political correctness gone mad". Nor did its economic policies involve "wasteful government spending". Tony Blair was not, as many gloomily or contentedly repeat, "a conservative in charge of the wrong party". Gordon Brown is not a conservative.

Nor is it the case that, if we have lost many others, conservatives have at least "won the argument over economics". The truth is that we have lost every argument at any level that matters. On all issues during the past quarter century or more, we have failed to set an agenda to preserve—let alone to re-establish—ourselves as the free citizens of an independent country. We have lost.

Now, I will emphasise that our defeat has extended over a generation. It was already evident before Tony Blair came into office. Undoubtedly, his Government did, after 1997, set records in this country for corruption and tyranny and treason. It increased taxes and spending. It regulated matters that even despotisms in other times and places have mostly left alone. It fought wars of aggression against Serbia and Afghanistan and Iraq, and justified these with the most shameless lies. It threw our armed forces into unwinnable occupations, and exposed us to attack by foreign terrorists and to insurrection from within the Asianised areas of our own cities. It hastened the transformation of our laws from a shield for the innocent into a weapon of the State. It placed us deeper under various kinds of foreign rule.

Yet evil as the Blair Government was, it was not original in its evil. The personal and financial corruption of the Ministers aside, its acts were entirely a working out of principles established before 1997. There was no break in continuity between the Blair and the Thatcher and Major Governments. It is notorious that no bad act of government since 1997 has been without precedent. We can ask whether Tony Blair was a Thatcherite, or whether John Major was the first Prime Minister of New Labour. The questions are equally unimportant. Our past three Prime Ministers may differ in order and degree, but not in their nature.

Nor is it important that Gordon Brown is now Prime Minister, or who may win the next general election. Electoral politics may change governments. It is normally other forces that determine the policies of government. Led by David Cameron, it is possible that the Conservatives will, before 2010, win office. But will this be a victory for conservatism? We can imagine a Conservative Government. It is much harder to imagine a government of conservatives.

Just as it is possible to trace the evils we now face over the past few generations, it is possible to look forward to a country—indeed, a world, for England is not alone—in which they will have triumphed. It is clear that our ruling class—or that loose coalition of politicians, bureaucrats, lawyers, educators, and media and business people who derive wealth and power and status from an enlarged and active state—wants an end of liberal democracy.

The desired new settlement that already exists in outline is one in which those at the top or with the right connections can enjoy the most fabulous wealth and status, and in which their enjoyment of these can never again be challenged from below. We, the ordinary people, are to be stripped of our constitutional rights—no freedom of speech, no personal or financial privacy, no procedural safeguards in the criminal law. We are to be taxed and regulated to what counts in our own culture as the edge of the breadline. This is on the one hand to provide incomes for clients of the ruling class, and on the other to deprive us of the leisure that might allow us to understand our situation, and of the confidence that might allow us to challenge it. In any event, every organ of the ruling class is at work on promoting ideologies of boundless submission to the new settlement.

At the same time, structures of accountability that emerged in the 17th and 18th centuries are to be deactivated. Their forms will continue. There will be assemblies at Westminster. But these will not be sovereign assemblies with the formal authority of life and death over us all. That authority will have been passed to various unelected and transnational agencies. And so far as the Westminster assemblies will remain important, our votes will have little effect on what they enact.

We are passing, in England and all over the West, into the sort of world that existed in much of Europe before the French Revolution—a world of diverse and conflicting sources of authority, all equally unaccountable. The great simplification of authority that happened in Europe after 1789, and that had happened over two centuries earlier in England, was a product of nationalism; and simplification was followed by accountability and then by liberalism.

This sort of reaction is in future to be made impossible by promoting movements of people so that nations in the old sense disappear, and are replaced by patchworks of nationalities more suspicious of each other than of any ruling class.

Seen as actors in an historic tendency, the Ministers of the Blair, and now of the Brown, Government are to be much condemned for their bad acts. But, as said, they really have only given a speed and individuality of detail to tendencies that were established before they came to power, and that will continue after they have fallen. The evils that we face are only partly a matter of individual wickedness.

To understand why all this has happened, and will continue to happen, we must look beyond electoral politics. We must even look beyond the ideologies, or claimed ideologies, of electoral politics. The true key to understanding lies in the analysis of class interest.

ONE: REVOLUTION FROM THE TOP

Government and the Ruling Class

Elected politicians never have the running of a country all to themselves. While undoubtedly important, they must in all cases govern with the advice and consent of a wider community of the powerful. There are the civil servants. There are the public sector educators. There are the semi-autonomous agencies funded by the tax payers. There are journalists and other communicators. There are certain formally private media and entertainment and legal and professional and business interests that also obtain power, status and income from the policies of government. Together, these form a web of individuals and institutions that is sometimes called the Establishment, though I prefer, in my present analysis, to call it the ruling class.

The Government is usually part of this ruling class. But this need not be the case. Short of a revolutionary terror to bring it to unconditional obedience, the ruling class is always autonomous of the Government. And there are times when the vagaries of birth or conquest or the electoral system will set the two in opposition. It is then, short of a terror, that the ruling class can block or slow the policies of a government with which it disagrees. It can even impose policies of its own quite opposite to those of the elected politicians. It can do this because of its size and permanence and its indispensability to every day government, and because of the cohesion it frequently gains from a shared body of ideas.

These ideas set the agenda of debate and policy. They determine what questions exist, how they can be discussed, and what solutions may be applied. They provide a whole language of debate. Ideas outside the range of what is established—and especially hostile ideas—are denigrated or ignored. They are seldom allowed full discussion in the usual media. Established ideas, on the other hand, are spread, through education and the general control of administrative organs, to the rest of the population.

Of course, this has always been the case. Even quite strongly dictatorial governments draw their legitimacy from consent—and perhaps the most important form of consent in the short term is of those who enforce their commands. Nor, in itself, is there anything sinister about an autonomous ruling class. As a repository of culture and experience, it can give a stability to government that unchecked political democracy may not.

In this country, however, the ruling class has become a sinister force. The immense growth of the State during the 20th century had already made it larger and more powerful than was healthy for liberal democracy. Already in the 1900s, the norms of limited government were giving way to the often arbitrary rules of an extended state. In the 1920s, the Lord Chief Justice himself could write of "the new despotism".[1] The tendency made enormous strides in the 1940s, with only a limited reaction in the next decade—a reaction sharply reversed in the 1960s. By 1979, the traditional forms of our Constitution remained in place, but were mingled with structures of extended power inconsistent with the spirit of our Constitution. These structures provided a living to millions—either through various kinds of welfare or though employment in the nationalised industries. Much of the formally private economy was corporatised and cartelised and regulated in ways that made it often another arm of government. Even without an ideology of revolutionary change, the ruling class had become a danger to our ancient ways.

Since around 1979, however, the ruling class has, in its commanding heights, been captured by people whose view of the world makes them not incidentally but fundamentally hostile to liberal democracy and all the other broadly conservative institutions of this country.

I repeat—this new ruling class is aiming at the establishment of absolute and unaccountable power. The establishment of such power may involve force. But much more than force, it involves a reshaping of our thoughts. This might seem a bizarre, or perhaps an exaggerated, claim. But it is true. The ruling class that we presently have is not satisfied with us as we presently are. It wants a new people over which it can exercise a new kind of dominion.

To see this desire in action, let us take several representative events—or classes of event—of the past ten years.

Stripping the Museums

In January 1999, work began on altering the exhibitions at the National Maritime Museum in Greenwich. It had until then been a place for learning about British supremacy at sea, and was loosely organised around the uniform worn by Nelson at the Battle of Trafalgar. According to Richard Ormond, the Director, it was "old-fashioned" and needed to change with the times. He explained:

> We're not spitting in our predecessors' graves, but when this museum was created the Red Ensign ruled supreme and as a maritime nation we were on the crest of a great wave. We are in a different world today.... Unless we find new intellectual purpose and bring home to people that the sea is still central to our lives, we will become a sideshow museum dealing with traditional artefacts to an increasingly limited market.[2]

---

[1] Lord Hewart of Bury (Lord Chief Justice of England), *The New Despotism*, Ernest Benn Limited, London, 1929.

[2] Quoted in "New look for the National Maritime Museum" *The Daily Telegraph*, London,

When someone says he is not spitting in someone's grave, there is fair chance that he is. Out, therefore, went most of the paintings and scale models—out too most of the displays about battles and exploration. In came exhibitions about slavery and history "from the position of the colonised". One of the new displays shows a white woman in eighteenth century costume with a manacled black hand reaching out to her. The text attached to this reads: "The slave trade was driven by the need for an English cup of tea".

There are also large displays about global warming, damage to the ozone layer, marine pollution, threatened fish stocks, and the "danger of rising sea levels". Commenting again, Mr Ormond made no apology for the change. Care of the sea, he said, was a "number one international issue". It had to be brought to our attention even if it meant reducing space for exhibitions about the past.[3]

Added to all this was a sprinkling of new works from something called the Sensation Generation of Young British Artists. Tacita Dean was commissioned to make a "video sculpture" about the sea. Stefan Gek had already made a sculpture by crushing a buoy in a diving chamber. There was a "Caribbean folk sculpture" suggested by the floats in the Notting Hill Carnival. And a video about weather forecasting was to use poetry and "talking fish".

These changes were unanimously approved by the Board of Trustees—one of whom was the Duke of Edinburgh; and the museum was reopened by the Queen the following 11th March. Commenting on this event, Mark Irving wrote in *The Independent*:

> In shifting gear from being a museum about maritime history to become a theme-park showcase for government-backed environmental projects and commercial achievement, the museum redefines our national image: "national', 'maritime' and 'museum' are words loaded with a special frisson.[4]

This was not an isolated instance of change. Since then, virtually all museums and galleries that receive public funds have been remodelled to weaken their connection with the past, or are being remodelled to make them into vehicles for contemporary propaganda.

The British Museum is a good illustration of this second purpose. Because the most celebrated of its exhibits are the products of alien and often dead races, and because the universal prestige of one of those races is such that only the boldest dare attack its works, this museum has not received the same comprehensive gutting as the National Maritime Museum. Instead, the labels

---

25th January 1999.

[3] *Ibid*

[4] Mark Irving, "Our past is all at sea", *The Independent*, London, 16th May 1999.

to exhibits in the Greek and Roman galleries have been supplemented by written comments by black people in this country about what those exhibits mean to them.

Even classical musicians have been told to change if they want to receive continued public funding. In October 2003, the Association of British Orchestras organised a symposium on Cultural Diversity and the Classical Music Industry, and effectively required attendance from every classical music organisation in England larger than a string quartet. Among those addressing the symposium was Professor Lola Young, Head of Culture at the Greater London Authority. She said: "We must change the look of the classical music industry".[5] She was supported by Roger Wright, head of BBC Radio 3, who confessed that everyone at the BBC now underwent "diversity training".[6]

The Secret Policeman

But the work of remodelling our thoughts goes beyond financial incentives. On Tuesday the 21st October 2003, the BBC showed *The Secret Policeman*. This was a television documentary in which a reporter posed for six months as a police cadet and then as a police officer, while secretly filming his colleagues. Some of the language caught on film expresses strong dissent from the established opinions on race and immigration. One of the officers put on a white hood and discussed the merits of burying a "Paki bastard under a railway line". He also insisted that Stephen Lawrence—a black youth whose death in mysterious circumstances led to a government inquiry into "institutional racism"—had deserved his end. He added:

> Isn't it good how good memories don't fade? He fucking deserved it, and his mum and dad are a fucking pair of spongers.

Another officer said of his Asian colleagues:

> Truthfully? Fuck them all off. I'll admit it—I'm a racist bastard. I don't mind blacks. I don't mind black people. Asians? No.

Another said of Asians in general:

> A dog born in a barn is still a dog. A Paki born in Britain is still a fucking Paki.

The documentary was shown to howls of outrage. The Acting Deputy Chief Constable of the North Wales Police said:

---

[5] Norman Lebrecht, "How the PC brigade is destroying our orchestras", *The Evening Standard*, London, 8th October 2003
[6] *Ibid*

I felt physically sick as I watched The Secret Policeman.[7]

The Deputy Chief Constable of the Manchester Police said:

I was shocked, sickened, ashamed and saddened by what I saw.[8]

The Home Secretary—at the time David Blunkett—joined in:

What's been revealed is horrendous. The issue is... what we can do to ensure police services across the country adopt the new training programmes on diversity to root out racists before they can get through the training programme.[9]

The Commissioner of the Metropolitan Police went further:

His force intends to plant informers in its classrooms to root out racist recruits. It will also allow community representatives to sit on recruitment panels to prevent racist applicants entering the force. At the Met's training school in Hendon, which trains 3,500 new officers a year, one recruit in a class will be secretly selected to inform on colleagues. Their identities will remain secret for the rest of their careers and they will act as intelligence gatherers. If racism is discovered by undercover officers, it may be used to provide evidence for a criminal prosecution for incitement to racial hatred.[10]

In other words, the Home Secretary was proposing to make political orthodoxy a condition of employment as a police officer. The Metropolitan Commissioner was proposing to set agents of provocation among his own officers.

Five of the officers filmed resigned the day after the showing. Another was suspended. What has happened since to them is beyond the scope of this work. But they will probably never again find the sort of employment that allows children or a mortgage. Their lives may have been ruined.

Doubtless, the words recorded were tasteless and uncharitable. But hardly anyone bothered to ask if the public reaction to them had not been excessive—after all, there was no evidence that those officers had carried, or were likely to carry, their opinions into acts against life or property.

---

[7] Jaya Narain and Adam Powell, "Five racist policemen quit force in disgrace", *The Daily Mail*, London, 23rd October 2003.

[8] *Ibid.* One police officer claims it took him over a week to recover from the shock of watching the programme. See Bryn Lewis, "Police racism is a challenge to the ethnic minorities", letter published in *The Independent*, London, 30th October 2003.

[9] Jaya Narain and Adam Powell, "Five racist policemen quit force in disgrace", *The Daily Mail*, London, 23rd October 2003.

[10] Helen Carter, "Informers will be planted at training colleges", *The Guardian*, London, 23rd October 2003.

The Dining Police

In fairness, though, the police are only preparing to do to each other what they have been occasionally doing to everyone else. In April 2000, it was reported that the police in Gloucestershire had formed a special unit to conduct what they called "Operation Napkin". Officers out of uniform were sent on weekend evenings into Indian and Chinese restaurants, their mission to arrest anyone who made impolite comments on the ethnic origin of the staff. This continued for a month, and was hailed by senior officers as a success—even though it had netted only one arrest.[11] Therefore, it was extended to Christmas. Chief Inspector Dean Walker, the officer in charge, confirmed that the operation would continue for the rest of the year. By now, one arrest had been joined by one caution.[12]

Success bred imitation. In March 2001, the Metropolitan Police launched their own offensive against "vindaloo and lager racism" in London. 25 officers out of uniform visited 10 ethnic restaurants chosen at random, in search of offenders. This operation was ordered by Deputy Assistant Commissioner Tarique Ghaffur. No doubt, Mr Ghaffur was concerned his officers should be given something to do in a city where theft and violence and general disorder were falling to their lowest points on record.[13]

The Homophobic Heresy

Not even high position in the Church brings immunity from the pressure to conform. Early in November 2003, the Bishop of Chester gave an interview to his local newspaper. He is a theological conservative, and is opposed to the ordination of practising homosexuals. During his interview, he said:

> Some people who are primarily homosexual can reorientate themselves. I would encourage them to consider that as an option, but I would not set myself up as a medical specialist on the subject—that's in the area of psychiatric health.[14]

Whatever we may think personally of homosexuality, or the ability or duty of homosexuals to alter their preferences, the Bishop was only expressing the settled doctrine of mainstream Christianity. The exceptional sinfulness of

---

[11] News report, "One held in Operation Napkin", *The Independent*, London, 26th April 2000.

[12] News report, "Police dine out on anti-racist campaign", *The Gloucestershire Echo*, Gloucester, 1st December 2000.

[13] News report, "Undercover probe into 'vindaloo racists'", *The Evening Standard*, London, 27th March 2001.

[14] Quoted in Richard Alleyne, "Bishop's anti-gay comments spark legal investigation", *The Daily Telegraph*, London, 10th November 2003.

homosexual acts has been clearly asserted since the third Lateran Council of 1179, and has at least some foundation in the Scriptures. Even so, he was immediately investigated by the police. The investigation came to nothing, but a spokesman for the Cheshire Constabulary commented:

> The issues raised have been examined. The Crown Prosecution Service has been consulted at length, and the Cheshire Constabulary is satisfied that no criminal offences have been committed. Current public order legislation does not provide specific offences based on sexuality.[15]

No further action was taken, but there was still a rebuke for the Bishop from the Chief Constable. He said:

> We need to be very aware of the position of minorities in this country and make sure diversity is celebrated. Vulnerable minorities should feel they are protected.[16]

No Platform for Weightists

As yet, there have been no prosecutions in this country for a deficiency of respect for those who choose to be different. But the authorities lose no opportunity to show the limits of their tolerance. In October 2005, Mary Magilton was run over in Oldham by a driver she described to the police as "fat". The Police, apparently, gave her a "frosty look" and told her to change her description. When she was unable to find a synonym for fat that came within their "appropriate language" guidelines, the police declined to take any statement from Mrs Magilton. The driver who ran her over does not appear to have been found.[17]

Bonfire of the Sanities

Then we have the 2003 Guy Fawks Night celebrations at Firle in Sussex. On the 25th October, the Firle Bonfire Society took an old caravan, put inside it effigies of a gypsy family, gave it the fake registration number P1KEY— "Pikey" being a term of abuse for gypsies in certain dialects of southern English—and dragged it in a procession through the village. They then took the caravan into a field and set light to it. Apparently, the onlookers cried: "Burn them, burn them".[18]

---

[15] Quoted in Matt Laddin, "Bishop's psychotherapy for gays comments not a crime", *The Independent*, London, 11th November 2003.

[16] Quoted in "Police clear Bishop in gay row", *The Times*, London, 11th November 2003.

[17] Brian Lashley, "PC's warning for mum who said 'fat'", *The Manchester Evening News*, Manchester, 13th October 205.

[18] Stewart Payne, "Effigies of gipsies are set alight at village party", *The Daily Telegraph*, London, 30th October 2003.

The caravan was private property, and was burned on private property. No one was injured in the event, and there was no incitement to acts of violence against identifiable individuals. Even so, the Commission for Racial Equality was involved within hours of the first—horrified—news reports. Trevor Phillips, its Chairman, said:

> This is clearly an example of incitement to racial hatred. You couldn't get more provocative than this.... [T]he matter should be pursued and the people involved punished... [to] prevent a culture that says discrimination and victimisation are OK[19]

The Firle Bonfire Society issued an "unreserved" apology, explaining that the event had been meant as a humorous comment on an eviction battle between the local authority and some gypsies—and that choosing topical themes for the annual bonfire was a tradition. But apologies and excuses were to no effect. By the 13th November 2003, the local police had arrested ten of those connected with the event. They were charged with offences under the Public Order Act 1986, which makes it a crime to incite "hatred" against any racial group. The maximum sentence on conviction is imprisonment for seven years. A police spokesman explained:

> The arrests are the result of a two-week investigation. We are taking this extremely seriously.[20]

Nigel Farage, the leader in the European Parliament of the UK Independence Party, intervened in defence of free speech. As a comment on the arrests, he announced his intention to set light to a caravan containing effigies of Edward Heath, John Major and Tony Blair. He was immediately threatened by the police with arrest for inciting racial hatred if he went ahead—politicians seem now to have been classed as an ethnic minority. Mr Farage had to content himself with comparing the use of 15 police officers to make the ten arrests with the 8,498 burglaries in Sussex during 2003, only 15 per cent of which had been solved. He said:

> It is amazing that lack of manpower prevents a higher clear-up rate, while 15 officers can be found to suppress free speech and investigate a politically correct crime.[21]

A Tale of the Little Pigs

There were no prosecutions of the Firle Bonfire Society. Nor was Nancy

---

[19] Quoted, *ibid.*
[20] "10 in gipsy fire probe", *The Daily Mirror*, London, 13th November 2003.
[21] UKIP News Release, "Police halt demonstrators by threatening arrest of MEP and staff", 13th November 2003.

Bennett prosecuted five years earlier for the similar offence of displaying china pigs in the front window of her house in Leicester. This had annoyed Moslems going past in the street to their local mosque. She had also annoyed them by decorating her house with union flags and putting in her window the Koranic text "Let there be no compulsion in religion".

In May 1998, the police entered her house under warrant and confiscated 15 of her china pigs. Then they submitted a report to the Crown Prosecution Service to see if she could be charged with any criminal offence. She could not be. But Yaqub Khan, speaking for the Leicester Federation of Muslim Organisations, made his feelings plain:

> There are rules which, as good citizens, we have to observe. We are a multi-faith society and we, as Muslims, respect other faiths practised in this country, so I think, in return, they should respect ours. Something like this is taken very seriously by Muslims and it is a very sensitive area.

> The quote from the *Koran* was also seen as provocative…. *The Koran* is a sacred book. If that is placed in a window where pigs have been placed then that is even more offensive. It may be a trivial matter for some sections of the community but it has to be dealt with.[22]

A Thousand Similar Cases?

Now, these are not isolated instances. They are not rare oddities or examples of British eccentricity. A reading of the national press will turn up sometimes dozens of similar cases in a week. And the daily newspapers continue to pile up similar instances. Take the case of David Davies, a Conservative Member of Parliament and the Member for Monmouth in the Welsh Assembly. In September 2005, he raised a laugh in the national media by submitting an application to the Heritage Fund for £48,000. He said he wanted to make a film about "the settled community". The joke in his application was that it closely mirrored the wording of a successful application to fund a film on gipsy culture. The joke was not found universally amusing. Mr Davies was reported to the Standards Committee of the Welsh Assembly. This body has the power to unseat him. A Welsh Nationalist Member of the Assembly accused him of

> Giving support to people who behave appallingly towards gipsies[23]

Then there are instances beyond counting in the newspapers of local authorities and schools that ban the wearing of Christian symbols, or refuse to

---

[22] Quoted in Claire Garner, "Police intervene in battle of 'offensive' china pigs", *The Independent*, London, 26th May 1998.

[23] News report, "MP accused over gipsy film jibe", *The Daily Telegraph*, London, 11th October 2005.

allow notice to be taken of the Christmas and Easter ceremonies—always on the alleged grounds that these "exclude" the devotees of other faiths.

A thorough search of the newspapers during even a few weeks might reveal enough instances of the tendency identified to fill an entire book. Certainly, searching an electronic database of British newspapers for the ten years to the 15th October 2006 turned up 862 uses of the phrase "political correctness gone mad". This is the phrase most commonly applied to such events. Perhaps many of these uses refer to multiple comments on the same event. On the other hand, not every such event attracts the phrase, and many others go unreported, or are reported in newspapers not in the database. This being so, it seems reasonable to suppose about a thousand similar cases over the past decade.

There could easily be more. The instances given above, then, can be seen as illustrations of a tendency. They manifest a ruthless hatred of the past, and an inquisitorial zeal for rooting out dissent. They show the nature of our ruling class as it has become.

There has not, I grant, been any abrupt change in this ruling class. There are still often to be seen the surface mannerisms of the old ruling class, and the personnel of the new are often related to the old. But there is, in all that matters, a new ruling class. This does not function as a repository of culture and experience. Nor—though these are important—is it primarily driven by sectional concerns about status and enrichment. It is instead a revolutionary class dedicated to the transformation of this country into something other than it has always been.

It may seem strange to talk about Marxist influence in an age when Marxism appears to have collapsed as any kind of revolutionary or governing force. But what we now face is best described as a Marxist revolution from above. It may not be the Marxism of Marx, but it is recognisably that of his followers.

TWO: THE MARXIST ROOTS OF THE REVOLUTION

The Neo-Marxist Rescue Hypothesis

According to Marx himself, the political and cultural shape of any society is determined by ownership of the means of production. There is the economic base, and piled on top of this is the superstructure of all else. Let the base be changed, and the superstructure will be changed as surely and automatically as the appearance of a forest is changed by the varying distance of our planet from the sun. There are inherent ambiguities in his theory and many possibly varying interpretations of it. But this summary is accurate enough for our current purposes.[24]

As here summarised, there is a rough grandeur to his claim. It is, however, false. We have now been waiting over 150 years for the inner contradictions of liberalism to reveal themselves, and so bring on the next stage of human development. There has been no immiserisation of the proletariat, and no general crisis of overproduction.

Aside from dropping the whole system as a failure, two responses to this problem emerged in the early 20th century. The first was to look around for some half-convincing rescue hypothesis—see Lenin, for example, on how exploiting the colonies had replaced exploiting the workers at home.[25] The second was a rescue hypothesis that kept the messianic fervour of the original ideology while dropping its discredited economic determinism. The three most important projectors of this hypothesis were Antonio Gramsci, Louis Althusser, and Michel Foucault .[26]

---

[24] In justification of this view of Marxism, see: "The Mode of production of material life conditions the social, political and intellectual life process in general" (Karl Marx, Preface to *A Critique of Political Economy*, in David McLellan (ed.) *Karl Marx: Selected Writings*, Oxford University Press, Oxford, 1977, p. 389).

See also: "[As the material production of a society develops, and men develop their material intercourse], so they alter, along with this, their real existence, their thinking and the products of their thinking" (Karl Marx and Friedrich Engels, *The German Ideology*, Progress Publishers, Moscow, 1964, p.38).

In general, it is often hard to say with any definiteness what Marx really meant. He wrote so much over so long a period; and his followers spent the hundred years after his death writing commentaries on his works, and then commentaries on each other, until the original was blurred like a landscape after heavy snow.

[25] V.I. Lenin, *Imperialism: The Highest Stage of Capitalism* (1916), Progress Publishers, Moscow, 1968.

[26] The works of these writers are often diffuse and hard to follow—see the general comment given above on Marxian scholarship. Rather than quote minutely from their work, it may be better just to provide a short reading list. In many cases, the editorial introduction gives a better understanding than the text that follows. See then: Antonio Gramsci (1891-

According to their reformulation of Marxism, a ruling class keeps control not by owning the means of production, but by setting the cultural agenda of the country. It formulates a "dominant" or "hegemonic" ideology, to legitimise its position, and imposes this on the rest of society through the "ideological state apparatus"—that is, through the political and legal administration, through the schools and universities and churches, through the media, through the family, and through the underlying assumptions of popular culture.[27]

There is some reliance on the use or threat of force to silence criticism—the "repressive state apparatus"—but the main instrument of control is the systematic manufacture of consent.[28] An ideology becomes hegemonic when it permeates the whole of society, determining its values, attitudes, beliefs and morality, and generally supporting the established order in all conversations and other relationships. Such an ideology ceases to be controversial for most people, instead being seen as common sense, or, even if undesirable, as a natural state of affairs. At times, it can amount to a "discourse", this being a set of ways of thinking and talking about issues that makes it at least hard for some things to be discussed at all.

It was because of this control through the cultural values of society—not through the use or threat of force—that the Marxist predictions of collapse and revolution were said to have been falsified. It was because the workers had been prevented from understanding their real interests by their acceptance of the dominant bourgeois ideology. Because they thought in terms of national identity and the amelioration of hardship through social reform, they could not see how exploited they were, and how no true improvement was possible within the existing mode of production.

Though much ingenuity has gone into proving the opposite, it is hard to see what value even a reformulated Marxism has for analysing the politics and culture of a liberal democracy. As said, there is a web of institutions and

---

1937), *Selections from the Prison Notebooks*, Lawrence and Wishart, London, 1971; Louis Althusser (1918-90), *For Marx*, Allen Lane, London, 1969; Michel Foucault (1926-84), *The Order of Things: An Archaeology of the Human Sciences*, Tavistock, London, 1974; by the same, *Discipline and Punish: The Birth of the Prison*, Tavistock, London, 1979.

[27] Anthony Giddens—who comes close to being one of the guiding minds of the New Labour Project—defines ideology as "shared ideas or beliefs which serve to justify the interests of dominant groups" (Anthony Giddens, *Sociology*, Polity Press, Cambridge, 3rd edition, 1997, p.583).

[28] "...the supremacy of a social group manifests itself in two ways, as 'domination' and as 'intellectual and moral leadership'.... The 'normal' exercise of hegemony on the now classical terrain of the parliamentary regime is characterised by the combination of force and consent, which balance each other reciprocally, without force predominating excessively over consent." (Gramsci, *op. cit.*, p.215)

individuals who establish and propagate certain ideas. But none of this has ever so far amounted to a hegemonic discourse. Rulers have tended to legitimise their position by reference to standards which were not imposed by them, but had largely emerged spontaneously throughout society as a whole. The function of the ideological state apparatus has been not to enforce values on the governed, but to reflect and thereby reinforce values already taken for granted. Even in times of emergency, liberal democracies have always been reasonably open societies, with a high degree of toleration of dissent, and economic institutions that had raised and were raising the living standards of all social groups.

The New Ruling Class

Nevertheless, while useless for analysing power within a liberal democracy, neo-Marxist sociology does apply to those people who now comprise the ruling class. They are self-consciously using an ideological state apparatus to impose their own, profoundly anti-conservative hegemony in Britain and throughout the English-speaking world.

This hegemony proceeds from the capture, over the past generation or so, of the ideological state apparatus. This did not begin in 1968, but that is the year when the strategy was first openly discussed in terms of a "long march through the institutions". The rioting of that year had not led to revolution from below: the hegemonic ideology of liberal democracy had too strong a hold on the minds of the workers. And so it was necessary for revolution to be imposed from above, by those able to reshape the terms of hegemony.[29]

We can see this in the domination of the universities by radical socialists. From Sociology and the other social studies, they spread out to colonise virtually every other discipline with the exceptions of Economics, Mathematics and the natural sciences. They are particularly strong in most departments of Education and in teacher training programmes.

Since the 1980s, Dennis O'Keeffe, now Professor of Sociology and the University of Buckingham, has been analysing the capture of education by the neo-Marxists. They dominate teacher training. They run the institutions, and they determine the modes of instruction. Student teachers are required to read and discuss and thereby absorb the works of Gramsci and Althusser and Foucault, among others. Professor O'Keeffe describes teacher training as

---

[29] According to Dominic Strinati: "The revolutionary forces have to take civil society before they take the state, and therefore have to build a coalition of oppositional groups united under a hegemonic banner which usurps the dominant or prevailing hegemony." (Dominic Strinati, *An Introduction to Theories of Popular Culture*, Routledge, London, 1995, p.169).

a missionising ideology. The world is [said to be] intolerable. It is full of unacceptable hierarchies. It is the duty of teacher education, at least so far as the school-world is concerned, remorselessly to combat these hierarchies.[30]

The neo-Marxists have been turning out generation after generation of graduates exposed to their ideas. Few of these graduates, of course, became committed activists. But, from early middle age downwards, there are now hundreds of thousands of intellectual workers—the key personnel of any administration—whose minds have been shaped within radical socialist assumptions. Even if they disagree with some of its practical implications, they have internalised the hegemonic ideology.

Looking at the beliefs, or the guiding assumptions of modern school teachers, Professor O'Keeffe finds that

socialist ideas pervade education....[31]

Leave aside those in the ideological state apparatus, and look at the leading personnel in the Governments we have had since 1997. Here, we see an almost unvaried hold on positions of importance by people whose minds have been at least shaped by the general ideas of neo-Marxist sociology.

Take Gordon Brown—a fervent socialist well into the 1990s. In 1975, he wrote:

The public control of industries is essential to the provision of social needs and services.[32]

In a longer work, published in 1989, he added:

The market cannot, unaided, educate and train our workforce, plan and fulfill national research goals or restore or even compensate for our battered infrastructure....And the market, unregulated, tends inevitably towards socially undesirable ends such as pollution, inequality and monopoly.[33]

Take Peter Mandelson—once a member of the Communist Party. Take John Reid—also once a member of the Communist Party. Take David Blunkett—on the "hard left" when he was Leader of Sheffield Council. Take Stephen Byers and Alan Milburn—once members of the International Socialists, now better known as the Socialist Workers Party. Take Margaret Hodge—as Leader

---

[30] Dennis O'Keeffe, *The Wayward Élite: A Critique of British Teacher-Education*, Adam Smith Institute, London, 1990, p.69.

[31] Dennis O'Keeffe, *Political Correctness and Public Finance*, Institute of Economic Affairs, London, 1999, p.49.

[32] Published in *Red Paper on Scotland*, 1975, quoted in Philip Johnston, "Does Brown have a doctrine for Britain?", *The Daily Telegraph*, London, 11th June 2007.

[33] Gordon Brown, *Where There's Greed: Margaret Thatcher and the Betrayal of Britain's Future*, Mainstream Publishing, Edinburgh, 1989, Introduction, pp.6-7.

of Islington Council, she flew the red flag over the town hall. Take Paul Boateng—once a "radical" black lawyer. Take Charles Clarke—he once boasted himself "further to the left than Wedgwood Benn".[34]

With the exception of Tony Blair himself—and perhaps only because he has never believed in any system of ideas—virtually everyone in or formerly in the present Government has an extreme socialist connection.[35]

They may not now be socialists in the economic sense. They have mostly shaved off their radical facial hair and have all now put on suits. Indeed, they are happy in practice to make deals with big business that they would once have denounced as fascist. But their most basic assumptions—from which their old economic analyses had proceeded—have remained intact.[36]

Marxist Theory is Marxist Practice

And this is what makes the various kinds of Marxist and neo-Marxist analysis so peculiarly appropriate to the actions of our new rulers. These analyses accurately describe how the minds of our rulers work. Speech in the old liberal democracies was reasonably free. There was an attempt to separate news from comment. Justice was fairly impartial. But since our new rulers spent their younger years denying these truths, they are quite willing, now they are in power, to act on the belief that they are not true. Because they believe that tolerance is repressive, they are repressive. Because they do not believe that objectivity is possible, they make no attempt at objectivity. Because they do not believe that justice is other than politics by other means, they are politicising justice. Because they believe that liberal democracy is a *façade* behind which a ruling class hides its ruthless hold on power, they are making a sham of liberal democracy. In this scheme of things, the works of a whole line of Marxist and neo-Marxist philosophers, from Gramsci to Foucault, are to be read not as a critique of liberal democracy, but as the manifesto of their students.[37]

---

[34] Quoted in Michael Gove, "The Marxist ideologues who are our masters now", *The Times*, London, 23rd January 2001.

[35] For America, see the career of Hillary Rodham Clinton. In 1969, she addressed her fellow students at Wellesley College thus: "As the French students wrote on the walls of the Sorbonne: 'Be realistic! Demand the impossible!' We cannot settle for less" (Boyd Tonkin, "Why New Labour is in search of an ideology", *The Independent*, London, 25th April 1998).

[36] According to Boyd Tonkin, "Yes, the folks involved [in New Labour] had long since dumped their faith in dialectical materialism, the vanguard party and the rest of it. What survived was a pattern-seeking, system-building cast of thought" ("Why New Labour is in search of an ideology", *The Independent*, London, 25th April 1998).

[37] And because they believe that business is ruthless and exploitative, they are ruthless and exploitative in their business dealings. They treat their workers like dirt, and conduct their

THREE: THE HEGEMONIC IDEOLOGY

Multiculturalism as Hegemonic Ideology

Let us turn now to the details of the ideology by which these people ensure cohesion of thought and speech and action, and by which they justify themselves to the ruled. It may seem that there is no single dominant ideology. There are different strands and emphases within the ruling class, and these often contradict each other. There is, for example, the passion to regulate where not ban every activity in the name of health and safety. There are claims about ozone depletion and anthropogenic global warming, and about the consequent need for all action to be regulated. There is the plan to join in a United States of Europe, and the late revival—though perhaps also collapse—of the old plan to join with the Americans in reordering the world. There is the present obsession with Islamic terrorism that is used to justify the creation of an overt police state.

These objectives cannot all be achieved at the same time. Several, indeed, are plainly in opposition. Nor is it always possible to judge motives. Do some people support the ban on tobacco advertising and the ban on smoking in "public places" because these come from the European Union? Or do they support the European Union because it is directing a war against tobacco? Hegemony is never a simple matter of one group with one agenda, but must be constantly negotiated between competing forces.

There is, even so, a commonality between the various kinds of hegemony. Obviously, all require an enlarged state. At the same time, whatever else it may be for, none has anything to do with the national past or the currently perceived interests of the majority.

Though it has not entirely broken with the past, and though it may appeal to tradition and popular aspirations as convenience requires, the ruling class legitimises itself on other grounds. And while there may be different strands and emphases, there is one strand and one emphasis that give the ideology its hegemonic nature.

This is the multicultural project. There are arguments over the details of the New Britain promised by New Labour. There is none over the fact that it is not to be a nation in any meaningful sense. Excepting only conformity to the hegemonic ideology, it is to have no homogeneity. It is instead to have "a rich diversity of communities". Some of these are to be sexual, some religious. But the real passion currently is for ethnic diversity.

In 1998, the Government set up a Commission on the Future of Multi-

---

affairs as close to naked fraud as their legal advice allows.

Ethnic Britain. Its purpose was

> to analyse the current state of multi-ethnic Britain and propose ways of countering racial discrimination and disadvantage and making Britain a confident and vibrant multicultural society at ease with its rich diversity.[38]

Chaired by Bhikhu Parekh, an academic placed in the House of Lords by Tony Blair, the Commission was a sub-division of the Runnymede Trust, a formally private body "devoted to promoting racial justice in Britain". Its Report can be seen as a digested expression of the transformation intended for this country. Among the recommendations were a formal declaration by the State that Britain was now a "multicultural society", and a commitment that

> deep-rooted antagonisms to racial and cultural differences [should be] defeated in practice, as well as symbolically written out of the national story.[39]

There was also some discussion of giving the country a new name:

> [The Name Britain] has systematic, largely unspoken, racial connotations.... Englishness and therefore by extension, Britishness, is racially coded.[40]

No new name was suggested, though it was emphasised that the country from now on should be regarded not as a community, but as a "community of communities".

Though elements within the ideological state apparatus have shown some willingness to incorporate them, the ruling class has yet to take full notice of these recommendations. But, its behaviour and language all proceed from the same assumptions. See the endless official fussing over criminal conviction rates and examination passes, the emphasis on "diversity", the careful blending of races and sexes and appearances in all official photographic opportunities, the changed emblems and mission statements of governmental agencies.

In the neo-Marxist terminology, the ruling class and its ideological state apparatus are imposing a new hegemonic ideology of multiculturalism.

---

[38] *Report of the Commission on the Future of Multi-Ethnic Britain*, published in 2000 by the Runnymede Trust—Introduction available at:
http://www.runnymedetrust.org/projects/meb/reportIntroduction.html (checked June 2007)
Published in hard copy by Profile, London, 2000.

[39] *Ibid.* See also in hard copy: "In the opening chapters of this report we have argued that some of the dominant stories in Britain need to be changed—stories about the past, the present and the future. With regard to the past we have recalled a range of myths: that the history of Britain goes back many centuries; that it has always been a basically peaceful and lawful place, un-troubled by internal dissent or strife; that there is a single true version of the national story; that until recently Britain was culturally homogeneous; that the sea round Britain aptly symbolises its independence and isolation from the rest of the world." (p. 103)

[40] *Ibid.*

A Cultural Project

To impose this ideology, it is necessary to destroy the old social order. Our new ruling class needs to overturn existing traditions and norms, standards and laws, history and heroes. Every autonomous institution, every set of historical associations, every pattern of loyalty that cannot be co-opted and controlled—these must be destroyed or neutralised. That is why the museums are being remodelled.

A nation is not merely the population of a territory. It also exists in time. People identify with each other partly because they live together and speak the same language and have similar customs and beliefs, but partly also because they have a common historical memory. Wiping this memory, as if it were a length of video tape, has become a priority of the ruling class. Great anniversaries from before 1914 are almost ignored. History in the old sense is no longer taught in state schools. The weights and measures have been changed by force. The names of every ancient form are changing. National and regional devolution is blurring the old constitutional landmarks. The stated justifications are all threadbare. No intelligent person could advocate them except as a means of turning the past into a foreign country.

Museums must be a primary target in this war against the past. They contain physical objects that real people once made and used. They help to tell us who we were and what we might be again.

This is particularly so with the National Maritime Museum. That is why it has been destroyed. The new Museum removes part of this physical link. True, Nelson's uniform remains on show. But it has been removed from the full context that gave it meaning. As the centrepiece of a museum filled with guns and scale models of Dreadnoughts, it was the secular equivalent of a saint's relic. As an appendage to a politically correct circus of modern art and moans about racism and the environment, it becomes at best a piece of blue cloth with a hole in it. At worst, it becomes tainted with all the sins alleged against our history.

Do this, and opposition to the transforming of the country will be neutralised. Strip us of our national identity, and we defend our traditions and freedom with all the confidence of an animal dragged from its lair.

But the project is not only about the removal of physical links. The overall strategy of attack is more subtle, if easily described. It involves controlling the language of public debate, control of the news and entertainment media, and the use of these to control perceptions of the past and thereby to shape the future. As George Orwell said in *Nineteen Eighty Four*, "who controls the present controls the past: who controls the past controls the future".

The Control of Language

Most obvious is the control of political taxonomy. The distinction between "right" and "left" is an extraordinarily pervasive force, shaping general understanding and judgement of political concepts. Hitler was on the "extreme right". Conservatives are on the "right". Therefore, all conservatives partake of evil, the extent of evil varying with the firmness with which conservative views are held. Any conservative who wants to achieve respect in the media must first show that his conservatism is of the "moderate" kind—that intellectually he is more of a social drinker than an alcoholic. Equally, libertarians and those called "neo-liberals" are on the "right". Therefore, they must be evil. The humorous accusation that someone is "to the right of Genghis Khan" serves the same function.

The use of this taxonomy allows the most contradictory views on politics and economics to be compounded, and all to be smeared without further examination as disreputable. Therefore, the "extreme right-winger" David Irving, who is a national socialist and holocaust revisionist; the "extreme right-winger" J.M. le Pen, who wants to reduce the flow of immigrants into France, but is not a national socialist and who apparently has much Jewish support in his country; and the "extreme right-winger" Enoch Powell, who was a traditional English conservative and a notable champion of liberal economics—all these are placed into the same category, and hostile judgements on one are by natural extension applied to the others.

At various times and in various ways, the trick has been played with other words—for example, "reform", progressive", "modernisation", and "outmoded". This first is among the earliest modern examples. From around the end of the 18th century, concerted efforts were made to alter the qualifications for voting in parliamentary elections. The advocates of change were arguing for the abandoning of a system that had been associated with the rise of England to wealth and national greatness, and that had allowed a reconciling of reasonably stable government with free institutions. In its place they wanted a franchise that had never before been tried—except perhaps in some of the revolutionary upheavals in Europe. Perhaps they were right. Perhaps they were proved right in the event. But their way was made easier by calling the proposed changes "reform"—a word they charged with positive associations—and leaving their conservative opponents to argue against "improvement".

Modern politics are less intellectually distinguished than in the 19th century. Therefore, less effort has been needed to play the trick with "outmoded"—which allows ideas and laws to be rejected simply on the grounds that they are old.[41] The word has a marvellous capacity to replace debate. Ideas and institutions are never good or bad, right or wrong: they are simply in or out of fashion. Since there is no arguing over fashion, there is no arguing over the things in or out of it.

Then there are the periodic changes of permitted terminology. Every so often, conservative newspapers report that a new word has been coined to describe an established fact, and laugh at the seeming pedantry with which use of this new word is enforced within the ideological state apparatus. For example, homosexual became "gay", which became "lesbian-and-gay", and which is now becoming "LGBT"—this being the acronym for "lesbian-gay-bisexual-transgendered".

Words and phrases like mongol, spastic, cripple, unmarried mother, and many others, have likewise been replaced and replaced again. In a sense, this is a misguided but well-meaning attempt to mitigate the hardship of the thing by finding new words that contain no added hurt. But its effect—and therefore part of its intention, a Granscian project being granted—is to remove conservatives from the moral high ground in any debate over policy on such people. When conservatives must think twice before opening their mouths, consulting their opponents on what language of description is now appropriate, they have conceded a very important part of the agenda of debate to their opponents. They have conceded an authority over words that must be gradually extended to a general authority. Conservatives may laugh at the clumsy acronyms and circumlocutions that are coined to replace existing words. But the intention is far from comic; and the effect is highly dangerous.

A similar effect is achieved with the frequent and often seemingly arbitrary changes of name given to ethnic groups and to places. Gypsies must now be called "Roma" or simply "Rom", and Red Indians must be called "Native Americans". Ceylon has become Sri Lanka, Dacca has become Dhaka, and Bombay has become Mumbai. Again, words are no longer the neutral means of discussion, but are charged with a political meaning, and judgements can be made on whether or not they are used as required.

---

[41] A random trawl of an electronic database of newspaper articles turned up these examples: "Peckinpah's violent and noble western is hot through with outmoded notions of honour and regret as the wild west begins to fade" (Television schedule, *The Guardian*, London, 17th November 2003); "I am neither militant nor a feminist but I have to say I still see no place in modern society for such outmoded misogynistic remarks" (Letter to the Editor, *This is Worcestershire*, Worcester, 19th November 2003); "And as for poor old W. Pollitt... and his outmoded thinking on parking policy...." (*This is Lancashire*, Lancaster, 17th November 2003); "...with Labour as the reactionaries fighting to defend the outmoded *status quo*" (Janet Daley, "Finally we can talk about policies", *The Daily Telegraph*, London, 12th November 2003).

Sometimes, words are imposed with a more immediate effect than forcing the deference of opponents. Take a word like "deprived", which has largely replaced the older word "poor". This came into general use in the 1970s, and was soon used without apology or comment even by Conservative Cabinet Ministers. It carries a powerful ideological charge—the message that anyone with money in the bank or a good set of clothes has somehow received an unfair advantage, and that those who lack these things have been deliberately excluded from the distribution. Though frequent use has tended to blunt its effect and make it no more than a synonym for poor, its acceptance in any debate on social policy puts conservatives at an instant disadvantage.[42]

Or take the use of "gender-neutral" language—the replacement of "he" as a general pronoun by "she/he", or "s/he", or "they", or by the random cycling of pronouns; and the renaming of just about every occupation containing the suffix "-man". This is supposed to make language more inclusive of both sexes, and is advanced on the grounds that it follows social changes that have brought women to a greater prominence than they enjoyed during the development of our language. This object could have been more economically pursued by allowing the pronoun "he" to take a neuter meaning unless a masculine was plainly required by the context. But this was probably not the main object of recasting the rules of composition. That was probably to draw a line separating the present from the past—to make past writings on almost any subject increasingly quaint, at which point, of course, they can be dismissed as "outmoded".

A similar effect can be seen in the compulsory metrication of weights and measures[43], in the changed names of counties and streets, and in the changed names of offices and institutions and forms—see, for example, the replacement of Lord Chancellor by Minister for Constitutional Affairs, of "writ" by "claim form", of "railway station" by "train station", of "Mayor" by "Leader", and so on.

Racism: The Ultimate Horror

Above all, take the word "racism". In this word, the ruling class has acquired a term of venomous abuse that can silence most criticism. That the word has

---

[42] See, for example, Isabel Oakeshotte: "New figures show the disease is no longer confined to deprived communities and is becoming a scourge throughout the capital" ("No one is safe from the spread of Tuberculosis", *The Evening Standard*, London 24th November 2003).

[43] That the metric system of weights and measures has many advantages cannot be doubted. Nevertheless, the advantages are not so great as to justify any amount of compulsion; and the circumstances in which use is compelled wholly outweigh these advantages.

no fixed meaning makes it all the better as a weapon of ideological control. It can mean a dislike of people because of their race or colour. It can mean a belief in differences between people of different races. It can mean a propensity to violence. It can mean no more than a preference for one's own people and values—even a belief that one has a "people". As "institutional racism", it can exist in the structures and assumptions of corporate bodies without the intent or knowledge of those employed within.[44] Or it can arise when every effort is being made to avoid it.[45] It can mean a mental disorder,[46] or a physical disorder of the brain,[47] or a sin.[48] It can even be stretched to

[44] On this point, see *The Stephen Lawrence Inquiry: Report of an Inquiry by Sir William MacPherson of Cluny*, HMSO, London, 1999, CM 4262-I&II:

"The collective failure of an organisation to provide an appropriate and professional service to people because of their colour, culture, or ethnic origin. It can be seen or detected in processes, attitudes and behaviour which amount to discrimination through unwitting prejudice, ignorance, thoughtlessness and racist stereotyping which disadvantage minority ethnic people." (6.34)

[45] *The Stephen Lawrence Inquiry*:

"Such failures can occur simply because police officers may mistakenly believe that it is legitimate to be "colour blind" in both individual and team response to the management and investigation of racist crimes, and in their relationship generally with people from minority ethnic communities. Such an approach is flawed. A colour blind approach fails to take account of the nature and needs of the person or the people involved, and of the special features which such crimes and their investigation possess." (6.18)

[46] See this from America: "Dr. Alvin Poussaint, a Harvard Medical School professor and perhaps the nation's most prominent African-American psychiatrist... urged the American Psychiatric Association [in 1999] to 'designate extreme racism as a mental health problem' by including it in its Diagnostic and Statistical Manual of Mental Disorders.....

"Poussaint gets support from Dr. Walter Shervington, president of the National Medical Association, an organization of more than 20,000 black physicians. When he took over leadership of the NMA last year, Shervington, a New Orleans psychiatrist, called for a discussion of adding racism to the APA's list of mental disorders.

"'When (racism) becomes so severe in its expression, should it not come to the attention of a psychiatrist or someone working in the mental health field in relationship to identifying what some of the core struggles are around it?' Shervington asks....

"Sabina Widner, a clinical psychologist who teaches at Augusta State University, is blunt about the human rights implications of classifying racism as a mental illness.

"'When I hear these types of things, I think about Russia,' she says, 'where people who are dissidents, people who don't hold majority views, are subjected to psychiatric treatment.'" (Extracted from John Head, "Can racists be called mentally ill? Debate strikes a nerve", *The Atlanta Journal and Constitution*, Atlanta, 23rd January 2000).

[47] "Scientists have developed a brain scan they claim to tell whether a person is racist. A group of 30 white volunteers were shown photographs of black individuals. Those with racist tendencies showed a surge of brain activity. That scientists reflected an attempt to curb latent racism.... This led researchers to conclude that racial prejudice exhausted the brain." (News story, "How a new brain scan can root out racism", *Metro*, London, 17th November 2003). See also Julie Henry, "Test to reveal 'inner racism' in job applicants", *The*

cover belief in the core beliefs of liberal democracy—after all, anyone who believes in the rights of the individual must also accept that some groups will have more successful individuals than others.[49]

It can mean any of these things or all of them[50]. Whatever it means in any

---

Sunday Telegraph, London, 10th June 2007.

It might be useful to know if the scientists can find any variation of activity in the brains of those who are happy to be racists, and to know why only white subjects were tested. On the other hand, it might not. Such claims made on the basis of 30 tests fall under the heading of "junk science", to stand beside virtually all the claims made against smoking and drinking.

[48] See: "The [Roman Catholic] church has come close to acknowledging the problem. Earlier this year, guidelines for parishes to review their practices described institutional racism as 'a form of structural sin and primarily a sin of omission'. (Stephen Bates, "Racism in Catholic Church 'driving minorities away'", *The Guardian*, London, 16th October 2000).

See also: "The Pope, clad in purple as a sign of penitence, said sorry on behalf of his flock for all past wrongdoings, from treatment of the Jews to forced conversions, the Crusades and Inquisition, and more contemporary sins such as discrimination against women and racism." (Frances Kennedy, "Pope confesses 2,000 years of Church sins", *The Independent*, London, 13th March 2000).

See also: "The Archbishop of Canterbury yesterday apologised for wars, racism and other sins committed in the name of Christianity." (Laura Clark, "Christian leaders say sorry for wars", *The Daily Mail*, London, 30th December 1999).

[49] According to Ann Leslie, writing in 1992, "[e]ven the word 'individual' can now be deemed as evidence of racism—as a student at Pennsylvania University discovered to her cost when she wrote a memorandum to the 'Diversity Education Committee' innocently declaring her 'deep regard for the individual'.

"The memo was returned with the word 'individual' heavily underscored: 'this is a red flag phrase today, which is considered by many to be racist. Arguments that champion the individual over the group ultimately privileges (*sic*) the 'individuals' belonging to the largest or dominant group'." (Ann Leslie, "The conspiracy to rule all our minds", *The Daily Mail*, London, 14th September 1992).

[50] In conversation, my late friend Chris R. Tame said this about racism: "Anti-racism is a useful ideological tool since the contemporary concept of racism is a portmanteau one, that combines a large—and apparently ceaselessly growing—number of quite distinct ideas. 'Racism' is used to describe or mean, amongst other things:

- the scientific view that important aspects of human intelligence and/or emotional disposition vary according to racial group and are transmitted genetically;
- the attribution to anyone holding such views that their belief is held on the basis of prejudice or blind hatred;
- that believing that there are average/general differences in IQ/emotional disposition between racial groups means that one hates other races, or seeks to deny them equal rights or just treatment;
- the denial of just, fair and meritocratic treatment to individuals on the basis of their race, ignoring their individual character, IQ or achievement;
- the practice of violence against, or denial of individual rights to, individuals of

particular context, it soils and discredits all who are labelled with it, placing them outside any claim to respect or tolerance or fair dealing. Modern English contains no greater instance of the power of words to terrify and subdue.

This explains the responses to the words recorded in *The Secret Policeman.* Look at the response of that Welsh police chief—he described himself as "physically sick" at what was said.

"Physically sick"? When was the last time any of us felt that about something read or heard? Cat droppings, rotten meat, certain medical conditions—these can set the average stomach heaving. But it is hard to think of anything written or said that really can provoke a physical response. And these were the words of a senior police officer. It has long been his professional duty to acquaint himself with matters that require a greater than average firmness of mind. "Physically sick"? It may be doubted.

But what those police officers said was not merely tasteless and uncharitable. Nor was it merely embarrassing to their senior officers. So far as their senior officers were concerned, and so far as the authors were concerned of virtually all media and political comment, what they said was the equivalent of heresy or treason. It was a duty not merely to deplore what they said, but to denounce it in the strongest terms that came to mind. Any faintness of utterance, it seems to have been felt, might leave one open to suspicions of agreement oneself with what had been said.

A similar trick is under way with the word "homophobic"—see that otherwise bizarre attack on the Bishop of Chester, and those otherwise scandalous comments of the local Chief Constable. But no discourse here has yet been established. It is still permitted to denounce the attack, and even to laugh at it. The event can be freely discussed. There is no need for deference to the overarching ideology, followed by dissent over its precise application. For how much longer this will continue, though, may be doubted.

Control of the News Media

Noam Chomsky, another radical socialist, is useful to an understanding of how the news media are controlled. There is no overt censorship of news—no bureau through which news must be cleared, no restrictive licensing of media outlets, no closed order of journalists, or whatever. Instead, only those journalists and media bureaucrats are ever appointed to positions of public

---

different races.

"As soon as we look critically at the varied meanings associated with the word 'racism' it is clear that one is dealing with what Ayn Rand calls an "anti-concept", a word designed actually to confuse distinct meanings and ideas, and to smuggle all sorts of unjustified assumptions into political discourse."

influence who already share the hegemonic ideology. They censor themselves.[51]

Again, the Chomsky analysis was intended to apply to the media in a liberal democracy, and was false. When liberal democracy was in its prime, there was a truly diverse media in which all strands of opinion found open expression. But, as ever, his analysis does apply to any media dominated by those he has influenced. Nobody tells BBC reporters how to cover stories. Instead, all BBC positions are advertised in *The Guardian*, and most are filled with graduates from the appropriate Media Studies courses.

Now, the propaganda thereby spread by this controlled media is not usually so overt as that of the great totalitarian tyrannies of the 20th century. Techniques of influence have much improved since then. News is reported, and with seeming accuracy. The propaganda lies in the selection and presentation of news.

To take a notorious example, everyone knows that the overwhelming majority of interracial crime in Britain and America is black on white. Yet this is not reflected in the media coverage. When the black teenager, Stephen Lawrence, was killed in South London back in 1992, the story received lavish coverage in the media; and the story continued through failed trials, a public enquiry, and the official and media harassment of the unconvicted suspects. The much larger number of black on white murders—known rather than suspected murders, and containing an obvious racial motivation—are either not reported at all or covered briefly and without comment in the local media.

Then there is the presentation of news. A skilled journalist can cover a story in such a way that no fact is untrue, and dissenting views are reported in full—and still manage to produce an article so biassed that it amounts to a lie. It is a question of selecting the right adjectives, or suggesting doubts or motives, of balancing quotations, of carefully taking words and opinions accurately reported but framing them in settings that suggest the opposite.

The greatest single exposure of these techniques is the 1993 article "How to Frame a Patriot" by Barry Krusch.[52] This almost by itself raises the analysis of media bias to an independent study. The article repays the closest reading. But, to give a brief example, look at the way in which almost all coverage in *The New York Times* and on CNN of the Oklahoma bombings include some reference to the American militia movement. No connection has ever been proven between the bombings and any militia, yet the connection is still made

---

[51] Professor Chomsky is an unusually prolific writer. See, however, his article "The Propaganda System", published in May 1992 in *Lies of Our Times*—available, with an archive of his other writings at *http://www.zmag.org/chomsky/index.cfm* (checked June 2007).

[52] Currently available, with an archive of his other writings, at *http://www.krusch.com*.

in reporting of the bombings—without making any overt accusation, the association is still made out.

Or look at the way in which nearly all media coverage of the British Conservative Party smuggles in some reference to the personal corruption of several Ministers in the John Major Cabinet. The exception to this rule is Kenneth Clarke, the leading Conservative supporter of British adoption of the Euro: his role in the arms to Iraq scandal is forgotten. Equally, any reporting of the far worse corruption in Tony Blair's Cabinet is usually accompanied more by pity than condemnation. Without any actual lies told, the impression conveyed is that the last Conservative Government was so corrupt that the known examples may have been a fraction of the whole, while the Blair Government—its war propaganda excepted—was a model of virtue compromised only by the Prime Minister's inability to realise that not all his colleagues reached his own standards of honesty.

Control of the Entertainment Media

Control of the entertainment media is an area almost uncovered in Britain, except for the radical socialist analyses of the 1960s and 1970s. But it is probably far more important than any control of the news media. Fewer and fewer people nowadays pay much attention to current affairs programmes on the television, or read anything in the newspapers beyond the sports pages—if they still read newspapers at all. But millions watch the entertainment programmes; and these have been recruited as part of the hegemonic apparatus.

Look at the BBC soap *Eastenders*. This is a programme in which almost no marriage is happy or lasts for long, in which anyone wearing a suit is likely to be a villain, and in which the few sympathetic characters are worthless but presented as victims of circumstances. While they may not have invented them, the scriptwriters have introduced at least two phrases into working class language: "It's doing my head in", and "It's all pressing in on me". These are usually screamed by one of the characters just before he commits some assault on his own property or another person. It means that the character has lost control of his emotions and can no longer be held accountable for his actions.

Then there is its almost comical political correctness. The last time I was able to make myself watch the programme, one of the characters was a taxi driver, and his mother in law an old working class native of the East End. Neither of them raised the obvious objection when one of his daughters decided to marry a black man—not that such a marriage would be in any sense wrong: what matters here is the deliberate absence of the obvious objection as part of a project of delegitimisation.

But this is a flourish. The longer term effect of the programme is to encourage intellectual passivity, an abandoning of moral responsibility, and an almost Mediterranean lack of emotional restraint.

Or look at the BBC Radio 4 soap *The Archers*. This is supposedly an "every day tale of ordinary country folk". It was this once. Nowadays, it is almost agitprop street theatre in its propagandising. Every male character is a monster or a weakling, or both. The female characters are pillars of feminist strength. The village pub is run by two homosexuals. The village solicitor is an Asian woman. A few years ago, the daughter of one of the characters brought back her black South African husband. His voice made it plain what he was: not one of the characters commented. There was virtually no discussion of the autumn 2002 Liberty and Livelihood march in London—the biggest rural demonstration since the Peasants' Revolt—nor did anyone attend it. All this is a small rural community!

Or look at how the BBC treats its own archive. Every so often, black and white footage of presenters from the 1950s is shown, with parodied upper class voices talking nonsense or mild obscenity added in place of the original sound. Is this meant to be funny? Perhaps it is. But its effect—and, again, its probable intention at least in part—is to sneer at the more polished and sedate modes of communication used before the present hegemonic control was imposed.

Together with what is shown goes what is not shown. In 1980, Benny Hill was told that his television contract would not be renewed. He was a very popular comedian in this country. In Central Europe, and to a lesser extent in the United States, he remains popular. But his humour was either not political, or was political in the wrong sense. It did not challenge conventional morality. Rather, it reinforced that morality while poking gentle fun at it. He was denounced as "sexist" because of his taste for scantily clothed young women. The more probable reason, though, was that he did not fit the agenda of the new generation that was taking control of television.

The same is true of the soap *Crossroads*. Though still attracting more than 11 million viewers, this was killed in 1987. Again, it was probably killed because of its cultural conservatism. The main character, Meg Richardson, was a strong and successful businesswoman. She was almost a character from an Ayn Rand novel in her facing of challenges and her ethical commitment.[53] Again, it was alleged that the programme had low production values. That has not prevented other programmes from remaining in production. Another culturally

---

[53] There was her frequent, and fondly recalled, assertion: "Prevarication is the thief of time". One might hear such words in *Eastenders* only from a character about to be arrested for cannibalism or marital rape.

conservative soap, *Neighbours*, is allowed to continue only because it is an Australian import, and because it is shown at times when hardly anyone is able to watch it. The adult soap schedules are dominated by programmes that are not conservative.

Or there is the killing, in 1981, of the old D'Oyly-Carte Opera Company. The Gilbert and Sullivan comic operas are glorious works of the English stage. Sullivan's music is some of the greatest ever composed in this country by a native. Gilbert's plots and lyrics are also works of genius. But the operas are also conservative—their celebration of values even as they poke gentle fun at them. And they were enjoyed by a generally conservative audience. The Opera Company had fallen on hard times, and had trouble maintaining its old production values. It applied to the Arts Council for funding, and was refused. It had to close. When at last revived, it had to limp along on whatever highly taxed private donations it could raise. Whatever may be thought of it in principle, state support has been made available for the most worthless travesties of art, so long as they conform to the anti-conservative agenda of arts funding. Gilbert and Sullivan were banished from the professional stage for years in this country because they did not so conform.

It is possible to fill up page after page with similar examples of the use of popular entertainment as a reinforcer of the hegemonic ideology—the careful balance of races and sexes in positions of authority, the vilification of white middle class men, the undermining of traditional morals and institutions, the general attack on all that is targeted for destruction.

Any one example given may seem trifling or even paranoid. But, taken together, the function of much of the entertainment media is to subvert the old order. Hardly ever are people told openly to go and vote Labour. But the overall effect is so to change perceptions of the present and past that voting Conservative or expressing conservative opinions comes to be regarded as about as normal and respectable as joining a Carmelite nunnery.[54]

Addendum

Since I wrote the above, the BBC has gone some way to admitting its systematic bias. In June 2007, it published *From Seesaw to Wagon Wheel: Safeguarding Impartiality in the 21st Century*.[55] This does not explicitly admit to

---

[54] Apparently, "American sociologists [have] discovered evidence that audience thinking could be positively influenced by soap operas: US viewers of medical soaps became convinced that more women were real-life doctors than was actually the case." (David Belcher, "A bubble that won't burst", *The Herald*, Glasgow, 28th February 2001)

[55] Available at:
http://www.bbc.co.uk/bbctrust/assets/files/pdf/review_report_research/impartiality_21century/report.pdf (checked June 2007)

bias. Indeed, it is filled with praise of the BBC as an impartial and respected source of information about the world. As an indictment of the BBC role in helping to create and maintain a corrupt discourse it is almost as bland as the various reports commissioned by the British Government into the war in Iraq. By concentrating mostly on the news and current affairs output of the BBC, it says little about the more pervasive use of entertainment as propaganda. Even here, it states fair intentions that there is no reason to suppose will be carried into effect.[56]

But its publication shows at least an awareness that others are aware of the bias. It means that my own—more radical analysis—cannot simply be dismissed as paranoia.

---

[56] See, for example: "Factual programming should not normally be built simply round a 'for' and 'against' proposition. Opinion is more complex and subtle than that. All rational shades of opinion should be covered, though not necessarily in equal proportions. Maverick or minority views should not necessarily be given equivalent weight with the prevailing consensus, but it is not the role of the BBC to close down debate. In both factual and non-factual output, there may be blanks on the creative canvas – sometimes caused by political correctness, sometimes by shared assumptions within the programme-making community, which result in the exclusion of uncongenial views or ideas. Filling in these blanks is a refreshing creative opportunity, and an essential element of impartiality." (*ibid*, pp.80-81)

FOUR: LEGITIMATION CRISES

Ideological Weakness

But even as the most senior functionaries within the repressive state apparatus strain both language and credibility in proclaiming adherence to it, the hegemonic ideology has one great apparent weakness. This is its impossibility. It is a false ideology.

It is possible for small alien minorities to be accepted into a country. Orthodox Jews are a good example. They live in the nation, but do not regard themselves as of it. What makes them acceptable is that they do not make nuisances of themselves and can never by their nature be other than a small minority. Even hardened anti-semites have little objection to the Orthodox, being more concerned about the alleged doings of the assimilated.

It is also possible for large numbers of aliens to be accepted into a nation so long as they assimilate and embrace its culture as their own. The United States in the century to about 1970 is a good case here. During this time, settlers of British ancestry went from being the majority to a large minority, but the American nation they had created continued to exist and to prosper by just about every reasonable standard. But a large and rapid immigration in which the burden of adjustment is thrown not on the newcomers but on the natives—in which, indeed, the newcomers are positively discouraged from assimilating—that is an obvious cause of resentment and even disorder.

There cannot be one society made up of widely different communities each of which loves and respects all the others. There cannot be a society in which the ethnic composition of every group—from university vice chancellors to hairdressers, from lunatic asylum inmates to fashion models—exactly parallels that of the census returns. Instead, there will be a retreat into ethnic nationalism among all groups.

In this context, the words of that police officer quoted above—"A dog born in a barn is still a dog. A Paki born in Britain is still a fucking Paki"—take on a grim significance. The words show a hardening of spiritual boundaries more typical of the Balkans or Africa than of the Britain we have always known—a nation of which membership has been more defined by allegiance to the Crown and adherence to certain norms than by race or colour.

Of course, the destruction of national identity will not make humanity love one another. We are pack animals by nature, and group loyalties will always survive. Destroy the customs and traditions that bind a people together, and a new cement of shared blood will rapidly emerge. What that police officer said is not integral to national pride. His words are part of what replaces it. Given such attitudes, most of our constitutional arrangements must tend to become

been something of a fraud in this country—and perhaps with good reason, as it is doubtful if the mass of people can ever be trusted with the vote. But rulers were vaguely answerable to the ruled, and could, given the right provocation, be removed. Multiculturalism turns us from a nation to which ultimately the rulers had to defer into a gathering of mutually hostile groups—all with different ambitions and complaints, all capable of being turned against each other in the manner that imperial ruling classes throughout history have used to nullify opposition. In the words of Margaret Thatcher,

> Thus the utopia of multiculturalism involves a bureaucratic class presiding over a nation divided into a variety of ethnic nationalities. That, of course, looks awfully like the old Soviet Union.[61]

Thought Crime and the Police State

And so we find ourselves living in a country where conformity to the dominant ideology is imposed by threats of force accompanied by an increasingly hysterical propaganda. It is as if the ruling class were waving a stick and turning up the volume on a television set—so it can stop others from talking about something else and give them no choice but to watch the programme.

And it is still not enough. Dissent has been driven out of the establishment media and out of respectable politics, but it continues to flourish in private and on the Internet. We live in a country where almost no one would describe himself openly as a "racist", but where the British National Party seems to stand on the edge of an electoral breakthrough.

Therefore the chorus of outrage when those police officers were exposed: there could be no public expressions of sympathy for them—indeed, the knowledge that there was much private agreement with at least the sentiments expressed, if not with their manner of expression, required the public denunciations to be all the more unsparing. It also explains the demand for still greater supervision of speech and action. As in some gentle parody of Stalin's Russia, it is accepted as necessary for conformity of speech and action to be so generally compelled that even the slightest expression of dissent stands out like a black swan among white.

This is the wider significance of the undercover filming of those police officers. It is worth asking why only white officers were filmed, when black and brown officers might not in private be oozing love and respect for their white colleagues. It is also worth asking in what context the words were uttered, and to what extent the reporter had made of himself an agent of

---

[61] Margaret Thatcher, "Resisting the utopian impulse", *American Outlook*, Spring 1999; quoted in "Culture, et cetera", *The Washington Times*, Washington DC, 22nd June 1999.

provocation. And it can be asked whether the opinions expressed could be shown to have had any effect on actions. But, while it would be useful to have some on the record, the answers are obvious. Witch hunts need witches. When they can be found in public, their finding must be ruthlessly used. When none can be found in public, they must be searched out in private. When none can be found at all, they must be invented.

However discovered, such dissent from the multicultural ideology can be used to justify its more intrusive imposition. Therefore, the promises of political tests for recruitment for the police, and of an inquisition to ensure conformity by the use of agents of provocation. Police officers are already bad enough. They are inefficient. They are incompetent. They are corrupt. But the known presence among them of informers and agents of provocation—can only tend to remove them still further from the rest of the population. They will become a sort of Janissaries, quite separate in outlook and perhaps in nationality from those they are employed to coerce into obedience.

Nor will covert information gathering be confined to the police. Once established as normal, it will be used against other targets. One of the recommendations of the Report into the death of Stephen Lawrence was

> [t]hat consideration should be given to amendment of the law to allow prosecution of offences involving racist language or behaviour, and of offences involving the possession of offensive weapons, where such conduct can be proved to have taken place otherwise than in a public place.[62]

This was rejected as unworkable. However, the use of undercover filming to gather evidence makes it workable. The informers and agents of provocation will spread into every area of private life. New friends or partners taken to dinner parties will constrain discussion even when no one intends to discuss the forbidden issues. We shall have to start learning the rules of private conduct that East Europeans have been forgetting since 1989. Life will become grimmer and more oppressive.

The Revolution was: The Terror is: Irreversible Change will be

We do not in this country face a revolution.[63] The revolution has already

---

[62] *The Stephen Lawrence Inquiry*, Chapter 49, Recommendation 39.

[63] The title of this section is suggested by the Garet Garret essay *The Revolution Was* (1938). See, in particular: "You do not defend a world that is already lost. When was it lost? That you cannot say precisely. It is a point for the revolutionary historian to ponder. We know only that it was surrendered peacefully, without a struggle, almost unawares. There was no day, no hour, no celebration of the event—and yet definitely, the ultimate power of initiative did pass from the hands of private enterprise to government." The whole essay is available on-line at:

http://www.rooseveltmyth.com/docs/The_Revolution_Was.html (checked June 2007)

happened. What we now see about us are its consequences, not its warning signs. We are entering the reign of terror that attends most revolutions. That no one has yet been murdered is unimportant. Terror is only incidentally about killing people. More fundamentally, it is about atomising any group opposed to the revolution so that resistance becomes impossible. That is the function of the otherwise random and bizarre persecutions mentioned above.

There may come a time when the repressive state apparatus will begin to operate with a Middle Eastern or South American zeal. At the moment, though, it is unnecessary—and the ruling class, for all it does or discusses, remains too much still under the influence of the old liberal democratic norms.

Because it was a cultural revolution, it was not marked by any great symbolic act of violence—no storming of the Bastille or of the Winter Palace. It came on instead in gentle stages, by the appointment of this person here to that position there, and by his commissioning of a new mission statement, or issuing of new instructions for the enforcement of rules already made.

The Labour victory of May 1997 was an important stage in the revolution, as it meant that those formally at the head of the executive no longer had to be led, in idleness or ignorance, along the revolutionary path, but could be expected to drive the whole machinery of state forward. But this was not the revolution.

How will all this end? Not, we can be sure, in Dr Parekh's "confident and vibrant multicultural society at ease with its rich diversity". One can reasonably see one of two outcomes.

The **first** is that the ruling class will keep control until it has finished remodelling the population. According to the 2001 returns—and these probably understate the truth—the non-white population of England rose by 40 per cent in the 1990s.[64] According to an anonymous demographer,

> Whites will be an ethnic minority in Britain by the end of the century. Analysis of official figures indicate that, at current fertility rates and levels of

---

[64] Paul Brown, "Minorities up 40%, census reveals", *The Guardian*, London, 4th September 2003. The official figures are:

England by Ethnic Group (000s)

	1981	1991	2001
White	44,682	44,848	44,925
Black	707	917	1,286
Asian	1,031	1,487	2,102
Orientals	414	626	825

immigration, there will be more non-whites than whites by 2100.[65]

With a small and credible adjustment to the extrapolated trends, minority status could be reached as soon as 2040. Long before either date, though, national life would have been wholly transformed. For ethnic change would not be accompanied by cultural assimilation. It would not here be as it was in America. No one called Kravitz sailed on the *Mayflower*. No one called Angelini signed the Declaration of Independence. Yet hundreds of millions who ancestors only arrived in America long after its birth as a nation now join in an uncomplicated celebration of its national rituals. Many nations have been connected by a common ancestry. But many have not, relying instead on commonality of allegiance or belief. Such is America. Such was Rome. Taking the English world as a whole, such has even been England.

Undoubtedly, the large differences of appearance shown by most of the newcomers to this country make the assimilation harder than was the case with the Huguenots or the Jews or the Irish. But they need not make it impossible. Many of our own newcomers have assimilated. But many have not; and the present and future pressures of migration, and the official policy towards migrants and their descendants will check—and even sometimes undo—the process of assimilation.

In these circumstances, ethnic change would not be accompanied by an assimilation in which white Englishmen were joined by black and brown Englishmen, and the nation went on much as before. Ethnic change would bring with it cultural displacement. Whole areas of the country would become alien; and within them, the physical appearances, place names, festivals, rituals and general customs of the past would be obliterated—in much the same way as happened when, from the 5th century, the northern barbarians displaced the Romanised Celts who had inhabited this country before them. Then, the ruling class could be safe. It would be presiding over an empire, not a nation, and would be safe from effective challenge.

The **second** outcome is that the English—or British—will turn nasty while still the majority. Probably this would not be an original nastiness. The French might well turn first, or the Israelis: We are not unique in the challenges we face, nor entirely in the nature of our ruling class. But there may come a time when the harsh ethnic nationalism of that police officer becomes the consensus. Then there will be a spiritual casting out of "strangers" from the nation, followed by ethnic cleansing of the strangers, and severe legal and social disabilities for those allowed to remain. And among these strangers will

---

[65] Anthony Browne, "UK whites will be minority by 2100", *The Observer*, London, 3rd September 2000. The demographer "wished to remain anonymous for fear of accusations of racism".

be many who are now unambiguously accepted as of the nation and who regard themselves as of the nation.

It is worth recalling that, until the National Socialists redrew the spiritual boundaries of the nation, many Jews were German nationalists. Such redrawing of spiritual boundaries would be just as much the end of what makes this country special as of the multicultural project itself; and no one who believes in liberal democracy can honourably lift a finger to help redraw them. But pious wishes will not stop their being redrawn if present trends are allowed to continue.

Either of these possible outcomes involves irreversible change. Each one closes the door on our more liberal past. But there is a **third** possible outcome. This is that present trends will not be allowed to continue, that the multicultural discourse will be overthrown before it is too late, that freedom of speech and action will be restored, and that private and public arrangements will be made to encourage assimilation of all British citizens to the cultural values of the majority. This will not bring us to Dr Parekh's land of harmonious diversity. But it is the only basis on which people of widely different appearances are ever likely to live at peace with each other.

FIVE: WHAT IS TO BE DONE?

Second Thoughts on Multiculturalism?

It may be that the failed war in Iraq has forced sections of the ruling class to think again. The terrorist bombings in London of July 2005. were a shock to anyone who believed that "diversity is strength" in our "community of communities". Reports began to appear in the newspapers of widespread disaffection among British Moslems—not only with the Iraq war, but also with the customs and institutions of this country.

In July 2006, for example, an official report drafted for the Prime Minister claimed that up to 16,000 British Moslems supported Islamic terrorism at home and abroad, while 416,000 Muslims felt no loyalty to this country.[66] All numerical claims of this sort are based on extrapolations; and without knowing the questions and methodology employed, such numbers are not to be accepted uncritically. But they do support much anecdotal evidence that some Moslems are less interested in joining in the multicultural love feast than in seating themselves at the head table.

To reports of this kind must be added discussions within the ruling class of a nature unknown since the 1960s. In November 2006, Jack Straw, Leader of the House of Commons, and formerly Home Secretary and Foreign Secretary, took up the long since rejected language of integration. "Simply breathing the same air as other members of society" he emphasised, "isn't integration".[67]

He was not alone. A year earlier, in September 2005, the Head of the Commission for Racial Equality said he was frightened that Britain was "sleepwalking its way to racial segregation."[68] Trevor Phillips, who had worked his way into the ruling class as an apostle of the multicultural faith, grew thereafter so keen on the promotion of "shared values" that he was eventually accused by the Mayor of London of trying to "move the race agenda away from a celebration of multiculturalism".[69]

Even doubts about the value of unlimited immigration can now be voiced within the ruling class. In October 2005, Polly Toynbee, one of the most

---

[66] The report, "Young Muslims and Extremism", was drawn up for the Prime Minister by officials at the Home and Foreign and Commonwealth Offices. It is reported in Sean Rayment, "Whites being lured into Islamic terror", *The Times*, London, 2nd July 2006.

[67] BBC News report, "Muslims must feel British—Straw", 2nd November 2006—available on-line at: *http://news.bbc.co.uk/1/hi/uk_politics/6110798.stm* (checked June 2007)

[68] BBC news report, "Schools 'must fight segregation", 22nd September 2005—available on-line at: *http://news.bbc.co.uk/1/hi/uk/4269988.stm* (checked June 2007)

[69] BBC news report, "Mayor's BNP outburst at Phillips, 1st September 2006—available on-line at: http://news.bbc.co.uk/1/hi/uk_politics/5301498.stm (checked June 2007)

notable propagandists of the ruling class wrote up her concerns in *The Guardian*. Under the title "It's not racist to want to control immigration", she spoke about the effect of immigration on working class living standards, and about the strain on public services.[70]

More recently, doubts have become explicit and voiced never the very top of politics. In June 2007, Ruth Kelly, the Communities Secretary, called on local authorities to encourage immigrants to learn English. She said in an interview given to the BBC:

> I think speaking the language is absolutely key. Something the commission looked at specifically is whether we should be translating from English into different languages as a matter of routine. They are going to put out guidance ... where local authorities can ask really hard questions about whether or not we are providing a crutch and supporting people in their difference, or whether translation is being used in the appropriate circumstances....
>
> I do think translation has been used too frequently and sometimes without thought to the consequences. So, for example, it's quite possible for someone to come here from Pakistan or elsewhere in the world and find that materials are routinely translated into their mother tongue, and therefore not have the incentive to learn the language.[71]

Hazel Blears, Chairman of the Labour Party and a candidate for its deputy leadership, went further. Speaking at the same time as Mrs Kelly, she accused immigrants of criminal and disorderly behaviour, of driving down living standards, and of changing the appearance of the country.[72]

But does any of this mean that the ruling class has seen where its policies are taking us, and is now having serious second thoughts? Undoubtedly, various realities previously overlooked or deliberately ignored have now become inescapable. But this does not mean that the ruling class or any significant group within it is considering the third outcome mentioned above.

Multiculturalism, remember, is not for our ruling class a set of abstract

---

[70] Polly Toynbee, "It's not racist to want to control immigration", *The Guardian*, Manchester and London, 11th October 2005.

[71] Quoted in news article, "Make migrants learn English, says Kelly", *The Times*, London, 11th June 2007.

[72] She said: "We have got areas in Salford where private landlords are letting properties with 10 and 12 people in there…. Now, the community doesn't object to the people—they object to the exploitation and the fact that that leads to people being on the street drinking, antisocial behaviour.

"They object if they are undercutting wages and not getting the national minimum wage and they are not abiding by health and safety, so you have got to enforce the law." (Quoted in news article, "Make migrants learn English, says Kelly", *The Times*, London, 11th June 2007.)

propositions to be accepted or rejected according to the evidence. It is an ideology that legitimises its power. It is a justification for jobs and status. It provides a shared language and shared values. It is to a large extent the social glue that holds the ruling class together. It is true that a systematic divergence between claims and reality will lead to the sort of crisis that destroyed Soviet Communism after about 1970. But we are far from seeing this for our own ruling class.

What we are seeing is a shift of rhetoric to pre-empt effective dissidence. If Labour Ministers start speaking like Nick Griffin, the electors may feel less inclined to vote for the British National Party. This is helped by the fact that perhaps the majority of recent immigrants have been white Slavs from the new member states of the European Union, and that complaints about their immigration can be insulated from any accusation of racism.

The effect of this shift in rhetoric has not been any moderation of policy. In the past few years, we have had new laws that make it a criminal offence to speak insultingly of Islam, an extension of the equality laws to cover homosexuals, and two attempts to send the Leader of the British National Party to prison for saying what until recently no one would have imagined might be a crime.

In return, we have been told that we can now fly the English flag outside our homes without seeking planning permission, and we have been promised "Britishness" lessons in the schools that will, in all probability, amount to more ruling class indoctrination. To balance this, we have had an immense sharpening of the repressive state apparatus, allegedly to counter the threat of Islamic terrorism, but almost certainly for use against all dissidence.

There has been no visible attempt to control the inflow of immigrants, legal or illegal. Nothing has been done to stop the inflow of asylum seekers. The enforcement of political correctness of the sort described above has continued unchecked.

A New Legitimising Ideology?

It may, however, be that, while the ruling class has no interest in formally dropping the multicultural project, it will become less important as a legitimising ideology. We are, at the moment, passing through the greatest moral panic of my lifetime. The media is filled with wild claims about the alleged fact of global warming, and the politicians are discussing law after law that are said to be needed if sea levels are not to rise by ten foot come next Tuesday. Almost every large organisation that I encounter is falling over itself to implement policies on recycling. Everyone in the news seems to be trading accusations about who is creating the biggest "carbon footprint". The schools and children's television are becoming little more than a giant evangelising project for the environmentalist faith.

Now, in principle, environmentalism is just as good a justification as multiculturalism for an extended and activist state. There are the same opportunities for demonising opponents, the same kinds of excuse for intrusive legislation. Is all this, then, an alternative legitimising ideology? Am I perhaps as out of date in worrying about multiculturalism as I might be in worrying about overmighty trade unions?

I think not. Despite the omnipresence of the global warming propaganda, environmentalism is attended by several important disadvantages as a legitimising ideology for the ruling class.

First, opposition at every level has not yet been stifled. No scientist has yet lost his job because he disagrees that the world is getting hotter, or that this is caused by our actions. The media still feels some obligation to treat the global warming claims as an open question. Because these claims and others like them are manifestly absurd, it would not be safe to rely on them while opponents were still free to laugh at them in public.

Second, claims about global warming still do not provide the same shared language and shared body of assumptions for the ruling class as multiculturalism and political correctness. Why change from a political cosmology that, with a few more epicycles, can be made to explain the world to one that has still to be fully developed?

Third, the business interests are not universally in agreement. Multiculturalism and political correctness can be absorbed by all large corporations as cartelised costs—that is, so that no important business interest suffers differentially. Environmentalism imposes significant and differential costs on much business. There are business interests that benefit from the panic over global warming. But oil companies, car manufacturers, transport companies, and many other businesses stand only to lose, and can be expected to resist more than token restrictions. In some cases, they can even be expected to fund opposition.

Moreover, when I say that the costs of environmentalism cannot be cartelised, we need also to bear in mind that the Chinese and the Indians, and perhaps the Americans, have no interest in sharing the burdens of environmental regulation. Whatever is done in this country, and in the European Union, imposes costs on local business that place it at a serious disadvantage with the rest of the world. This requires government to consider either much higher levels of protectionism than are currently fashionable, or a steady outflow of investment and jobs.

Fourth, environmentalism imposes direct and obvious costs on ordinary people. The current legitimising ideology imposes such costs only on a minority. We are all oppressed and impoverished. But only a few at any one time have this brought inescapably to their attention. Environmentalism, on the other hand, raises food and transport costs, reduces consumer choice, and forces people to recycle or to live without forms of waste disposal formerly taken for granted. It is politically unpopular whenever translated from hysterical propaganda to meaningful action. Witness, as an instance of this, the recent electoral revolt against councils that wanted to abolish weekly rubbish collections.

And environmentalism does not hold out any promise of a better world. Politically correct multiculturalism may be taking us towards a nightmare of universal surveillance and dispossession. But the formal promise is one of fairness for all. The best the environmentalists have to offer is a tightening of belts

For these reasons, I do not yet think there is to be a change of legitimising ideology. In medical terms, environmentalism is still to be seen as a secondary infection. The totalitarian hysteria with which it is currently accepted is more a symptom of ruling class control than a main excuse. Like the mania against smoking and obesity and vicious dogs and weapons of self-defence, it could never have been made into an excuse for jobbery and oppression except in a nation already morally disarmed.

I may be wrong. But I predict that claims about global warming will sooner or later go the way of claims about ozone depletion. They will not go away. At the same time, they will cease to be any positive guide to action. It is unlikely that the ruling class has lost faith in the multicultural project as a legitimising ideology.

The Quisling Right

What, then, of the Conservative Party? Is this not opposed to political correctness? Is this not the party of continuity with the past? The answer is no, it is not. There is no reason to suppose that the third of our outcomes will be promoted by the next Conservative Government.

Let us assume for the moment that the strategists of the Conservative Party are right—that Gordon Brown will be a less able opponent than Tony Blair was—and let us assume that a Conservative Government led by David Cameron will be a government of conservatives. The first of these assumptions has not so far been tested, and the second is manifestly unlikely. But let us make them. How, then, would such a government be able even to rule the country, let alone reverse the harm of the past few decades, with an ideological state apparatus so heavily politicised and so heavily biassed against them?

One answer is that it would not be able. It is not true that an election battle in the country is all that needs to won, and that after this, the decision of the people will be accepted. We can be sure that any such decision will not be accepted. Given the personnel of the ideological state apparatus—and increasingly of the repressive state apparatus—it would be absurd to imagine that the present cultural revolution would be called off because of a small and perhaps temporary change at the top. This is a Gramscian project carried out by Gramscians. These people spent their younger years reading and thinking about ideological hegemony, and they are now, in their middle years, trying to achieve it.

I will shortly move to a discussion of what a government of conservatives might do to win the culture war. But I have spoken in private with many Conservative Members of Parliament and advisers to the Conservative leadership. None of these people has given me reason to suppose he even understands the nature of what has been done. There has certainly been no proper thought given to a response. The best of these people have been waiting for the past decade for Labour to renationalise British Telecom. They read their economics in the 1980s, and this is an argument they might win. But since Labour has moved away from socialism in the old sense, this fluency in economic debate has been useless.

That is so for the more genuinely conservative of the Conservatives. The Party, however, is dominated by people who are not conservatives at all. The fuller answer to the question of whether the next Conservative Government will halt the revolution before it reaches the point of no return is that it will not—because it will not want to.

In government, the Conservatives would not even try to challenge the project of our ruling class. The Conservatives ruled this country between 1979 and 1997, and there was no break in continuity between where they left off and the Blair Government began. The difference between a Conservative and a Labour Government after the next election, it must be accepted, would be one of tone rather than of substance.

For as long as I have been alive—and for some while before—the Conservative Party has been a gigantic fraud on the people of this country. Its true function has not been to articulate, but to neutralise discontent. The only threat to the hegemony of the ruling class has been the deeply conservative prejudices of the English people. Any conservatism would be a threat, because it means an adherence to values not fully controlled by the ruling class. English conservatism, though, is an especially dangerous threat. Its values are those of a roughly libertarian past—of self-reliance, of patriotism, of a vague belief that while government may often be useful, it is not fundamentally necessary, and is never wholly to be trusted.

The answer has been a Conservative Party that is not really conservative. It has so far been necessary in England for at least the appearance of representative government and a free press to be maintained. That means allowing a Conservative Party and an associated media. But these must be heavily policed at all times, so that nothing very conservative is ever done.

This policing is done *via* what may be called the Quisling Right. These are the equivalent of the people who used to run the Social Democratic Parties and the semi-tolerated churches in the better parts of the Soviet Empire. They have status and income from maintaining the appearance of a pluralism that does not really exist. They accept the new hegemony while keeping up a pretence of opposing it.

These people run the Conservative Party. They are heavily clustered in *The Daily Telegraph* and in *The Spectator*. They are strategically scattered through other conservative bodies and institutions—not always in positions of overt power, but always in positions of quiet influence.

I must say here that I am not claiming some grand conspiracy. I do not think there has been any deliberate coordination. As anyone knows who has studied Economics or the natural sciences, the world is filled with regularities of structure and behaviour that seem to prove some hidden designer, but that can be explained by purely secondary causes.

So it is with the Quisling Right. Ambitious and unprincipled people have seen a demand among the public for a conservative opposition. At the same time, they have understood the permitted boundaries of opposition. They have known that anyone who makes a serious challenge to the power of the ruling class will be utterly destroyed by it.

Their response has been a balancing of forces. They have wanted office, and therefore have had to keep people voting for the Conservative Party. They are quite happy not to be in control of the car, so long as they can be comfortably seated in the back. To achieve this, they will make strongly conservative noises in opposition, but always imply action without promising, or promise without delivering. Their object is to use the discontent of large bodies of opinion to get into office, and then be careful not to transgress the permitted boundaries.

The reward for being a good Quisling Rightist is to be allowed to seek election to office, without alienating the Enemy Class. He will be denounced—but with none of the force and venom reserved for people like Enoch Powell and Margaret Thatcher. For all the public hostility he faces, he will be fully accepted in private. He will remain welcome at the Aldeburgh Festival and the smart dinner parties. He will be invited on to programmes like *Question Time*, and even get to make the occasional programme of his own. He will be awarded honorary degrees from the good universities. He will be able eventually to retire into some nice business or media or academic sinecure. In short, he will be given personal success and a standing advantage over less compliant rivals. He can have all this, so long as at the right moment he always betrays those who voted for him.

This is why, despite long periods of electoral dominance by the Conservative Party, the past 60 years have been so generally disastrous in England for the linked causes of freedom and tradition. The leaders of that Party have specialised in putting on an impressive *charade* of conservatism without achieving a single conservative end. In the early days, nothing was done to stop—let alone turn back—the advance of socialism. More recently, nothing has been done against the attempted smashing of the English cultural identity.

What the Quisling Right has achieved is the political equivalent of decaffeinated coffee. It has the same aroma and the same taste, and it requires the same rituals of making and drinking. It only lacks the effect that makes it worth bothering with in the first place.[73]

We saw this clearly in the leadership of William Hague. When it failed to convince, the Conservative Party went through the brief *interregna* of Iain Duncan Smith and of Michael Howard. So far as anything has changed under David Cameron, it has been the partial dropping of the Quisling Rightist pose in favour of a more frank acceptance of the established order of things. The belief among Conservative strategists appears to be that Conservative voters are now so desperate to be rid of Labour, that there is no need to court them: all effort can therefore go into conciliating the ruling class in advance of victory. Had any of the three previous Conservative leaders won a general election, promises actual or implied would have been broken in office. Mr Cameron has not even bothered with such promises.

Nothing can be expected of the next Conservative Government.

What is to be Done?

What, then, is to be done? Perhaps the true answer is nothing. Perhaps the revolution is already beyond reversal. Perhaps the only salvation for ourselves and our families is to get out of this country while the Pound remains high on the foreign exchanges, and while there are no controls on the export of capital. England is not the only country passing through this transformation. But it is undoubtedly in the vanguard. It is more fully than most other countries under

---

[73] For an example of Conservative fraudulence, see Appendix One.

the rule of a revolutionary class, and it still has a sufficiently honest and competent administration for revolutionary transformation to affect every household. There are many other parts of the world where little so far has changed, or where foreign residents, possessed of capital, will not be disturbed so long as they are politically inactive.

In the past decade or so, around five million people have left this country. Perhaps we should join them.

On the other hand, the fact that we stay here, indicates that we are patriotic enough to want to fight until we have unambiguously lost. For the moment, the revolution may not be irreversible. The correlation of forces may appear disastrous. But the forces of conservatism have not yet been utterly defeated.

This being so, let us explore how, even at this advanced stage, the revolution against our freedom and our national identity might be broken—how the ruling class might, at its very moment of triumph, be smashed, and held from any recovery of strength for two or three generations to come.

We face a ruling class, confident in its ideology, entrenched in all the governing institutions, unwavering in the advancement of its agenda. How can we even contemplate a reaction against all that it has achieved and is planning to achieve?

In the technical sense, there is no problem. There is one institutional weakness of the ruling class. It is large. It is diverse. It can accommodate endlessly various emphases of purpose. But it also overwhelmingly draws income and status from a single source—the State. Its attack on us is like the many different jets of water from a shower head. Yet, as with a shower head, its entire force is regulated by a single tap. Whoever can seize control of that tap controls the dependent force.

The ruling class may be able to frustrate the positive agenda of an opposed government. But it has no defence against a purely negative agenda. What needs to be done, therefore, is obvious. It is what the Marxists call a frontal attack.

A Frontal Attack

Let us assume for the sake of argument that we can seize power. How we might achieve this I will not for the moment discuss. It is enough to assume that we can gain a majority of the seats in the House of Commons and form a government in the normal way. Let us further assume a ruthless counter-revolutionary purpose. We are determined on a policy of reaction—that is, to undo all the bad acts of the last twenty governments or so in this country, and to destroy the institutional bases of our class enemy. Granting all this, let us see what ought to be done.

I begin by explaining what should not be done. Frontal attacks do not involve moderation. We do not accept any need in the short term for conciliating the ruling class. In its more hopeful days, the Thatcher Government tried this. Back then, even the better Ministers thought they were members of this class, and tried persuading it, and playing it off one faction against the other. We could try the same, in the hope that the Internet and the decline of its legitimising ideologies would one day reduce its power.

The problem with this approach is that it carries a high risk of failure. If we wait for any natural decline of the ruling class, it may not leave us with very much to save. Also, it might well prove less reasonable with us than it often did in the 1980s—then, after all, it was divided over economic policy. We might find it flatly opposed to everything we wanted to do.

Certainly, it would resist withdrawal from the European Union. We would have to face down an army of interest groups, all with privileged access to the media. If we did get our way, we would be hounded with every adverse statistic and comparison that could be constructed. We would eventually lose power to a government controlled by the ruling class that would hold a referendum every two years until the country rejoined.

And this would happen on one of the core issues of the conservative movement. On other issues, it might not matter what mandate we could show. Our Government would exist on sufferance.

No—my counsel is for open war. Moderation has its place, but not here. If we ever seize power, by whatever means, it will give us one chance of victory. Defeat will be followed by no second chance. Given control of the House of Commons, I would not bother seeing the present ruling class as an unavoidable ally in government. I would regard it as Margaret Thatcher did the unions—as an enemy crying out to be smashed.

Smashing the Class Enemy

I suggest, therefore, that within days of coming into power, we ought to shut down large parts of the public sector. We should abolish the Foreign Office, the Department of Trade and Industry, the Department of Culture, Media and Sport, the Department of Education and Training, the Ministry of Agriculture, Fisheries and Food, plus whole divisions of other ministries. We should shut down most of local government—especially anything to do with child welfare, consumer protection, racial equality, and town and country planning.

At the same time, we should abolish all the statutory agencies. This includes English Heritage, the Arts Council, the Commission for Racial Equality, the Equal Opportunities Commission, the Health and Safety Executive, whatever has replaced the Health Education Authority, the Serious Fraud Office, the

National Criminal Intelligence Service, all the regional development councils, and all the "self-financing regulatory agencies" without exception.

The fact that I have mentioned some organisations and not others does not indicate that these others are to be saved: the schedule to our Act of Abolition and Repeal should run to hundreds of pages. We should abolish functions, destroy records, sell off physical assets, and sack people by the tens of thousand. Pension rights could be respected according to law, but at least a third of government should no longer exist after our first month in power.

The chief purpose of what I suggest is not to save money for the taxpayers, or to free them from a bureaucratic tyranny. Though libertarians will think these desirable ends, and though they will undoubtedly prove beneficial after a few initial difficulties, they do not commend themselves equally to all sections of our movement, some of which will think more about the difficulties than the benefits. *The chief purpose is to destroy the present ruling class.*

Moving as fast as we can, we must abolish as much as we can of its institutional means of action and support.[74]

What makes a sinking ship such good drama is the collapse of hierarchy and every other relationship that it sometimes involves. The connections that normally hold people to each other in effective groups are severed, and what was a stable society is dissolved into a terrified mob—some fighting desperately to get into the few lifeboats, others clinging to broken spars, others drowning in quiet despair. That is what we should be planning to do to the present ruling class.

Dealing with one institution at a time sounds the more sensible and moderate approach. In fact, it would only lead to a series of set piece battles, in every one of which the enemy could deploy its full weight against us. The general shipwreck that I suggest is far more likely to succeed. People who are on the dole, or working 14 hours a day in telesales to pay mortgages—and whose friends and contacts are nearly all in the same position—will have lost their ability to oppose or delay us. Their verbal opposition, though loud, would be no louder than if we did nothing. So long as we kept our heads, any

---

[74] Karl Marx himself would have agreed. Writing in April 1871, he declared that "the next attempt of the French Revolution will be no longer, as before, to transfer the bureaucratic-military machine from one hand to another, but to *smash* it, and this is the precondition for every real people's revolution...."(Quoted in V.I. Lenin, *The State and Revolution* (1917), Chapter 3—available at:
  http://www.marxists.org/archive/lenin/works/1917/staterev/ch03.htm (checked June 2007))
He and his followers are useful not only for analysing the situation in which they have placed us, but also for suggesting the means by which it can be reversed. The declared objects of their revolution were always unattainable. But their close study of revolutions is to be respected. We must smash the present ruling class, and replace it with one of our own.

violence could be easily suppressed.

Nor do I think there would be much procedural opposition. Once we were out of the European Union—our very first public act—the courts would again be subordinate to the Queen in Parliament: we could legislate, relegislate, and legislate again to get our way. As for the new House of Lords, it has no legitimacy as an upper house, and we should make sure to pack it with our own supporters. We could win.

The BBC and Other Media

The same considerations should guide our media policy. We should take the BBC permanently off air. I accept that it has existed long enough and been prominent enough to qualify as an historic institution. I also accept that, bias aside, it probably is the best broadcasting organisation in the world. But I see no alternative to shutting it down.

Anyone who thinks it can be captured and firmly governed by our people is dreaming. There are not enough of us with the necessary technical and managerial skills. At best, we might put a few of our people at the top—only to see them bypassed or marginalised. Besides, the hegemonic function of the BBC is not confined to its programming. It also gives employment to people who might under our management be scrupulously impartial, but who would continue using their status and contacts to fight us in other media.[75]

Nor do I think privatisation a good idea. As said, the BBC is a great broadcasting organisation. Freed from state control, it might easily grow larger and richer and more powerful. This would not necessarily diminish its function as a propaganda tool for the present ruling class—look at CNN and the other American networks. Therefore, it must be destroyed, its copyrights transferred to a successor company for licensing to other broadcasters.

Turning to these other broadcasters, we should as a matter of course abolish all the licensing and regulatory bodies that presently guide their activities. This would destroy more ruling class jobs and power, and allow viewers to get more of the programmes they really wanted. It would also lead to a rapid expansion of private broadcasting, in which many of the sacked from the BBC would find new jobs.

I see no reason here for concern: moved into different cultural environments, people often behave differently. Even if some present ruling class influence did remain, it would not be our business to intervene further.

---

[75] A good example of this, admitted by the BBC itself, is the endorsement of Hillary Clinton as a candidate for the American Presidency by Jeremy Vine, a prominent news presenter. See Jeremy Vine, "Why the world needs Hillary", *The Daily Mirror*, London, 22nd January 2007.

Our media policy should be to destroy a hegemonic grip, not establish one of our own.

That is why I will say nothing about the newspapers. What they choose to publish is beyond the normal sphere of government concern. This being said, it would be interesting to see how long *The Guardian* stayed in business without its daily subsidy from advertising jobs in the public sector.

Education

Our education policy would need to be more complex. On the one hand, we should cut off all state funding to the universities. We might allow some separate transitional support for a few science departments. But we should be careful not to allow another penny of support for any Economics or Law or Sociology or Government and Politics department, or for any course with the words "media", "gender", or "ethnicity" in its name. Doubtless, many students would be upset to lose their chance of getting a degree; but we could find some compensation for them—and, bearing in mind the mixture of worthless knowledge and ruling class indoctrination from which we would be saving them, they would not suffer on balance.

On the other hand, we would have to keep the schools open—not because their teaching is needed, but because of their childminding function. Most people would neither notice nor care about losing things like the Committee on Medical Aspects of Food Policy, but they would object to having to find somewhere else to put their little ones during the day.

Therefore, the schools would stay open. The compulsory attendance laws would be abolished, and encouragement given to the founding of independent schools—a voucher scheme might be useful here. All teacher training colleges would be closed, and the removal of formal hiring privileges would make their qualifications worthless. But state education would continue for the moment. The schools in each area would be put under the absolute rule of boards of guardians. These would be chosen by lot from qualified candidates, and empowered to collect a local rate to pay for their activities. The purpose here is not to improve state education—though that could easily be the effect—but to insulate it from the displaced ruling class and its satellite interests. This is also the purpose of avoiding elections to the boards—as these would soon be corrupted by organised minorities.

The Welfare State

Something we should leave substantially alone is the welfare state. The main assumption behind which the present ruling class justifies its looting of the taxpayers is that any cuts in public spending must fall on the welfare budget.

Of course, it is a false assumption, but it does not help that libertarians have always made a great noise about the corrupting effects of state welfare, and that libertarian schemes of improvement always give prominence to privatising or abolishing it. This shows a failure of political understanding.

All else aside, it would be madness to give the now displaced ruling class an issue on which it might claw its way back from oblivion. It may be regrettable, but most people in England like welfare. They like the thought that if they lose their jobs, they will receive some basic support, and that if they fall ill, they will receive treatment free at the point of use. That is what is wanted, and that is what a government of reaction must continue providing.

It need not actually be very expensive. Most people would rather work than claim; and in a free economy, there would be no lack of work. As for the National Health Service, the main expenses here come from structures that currently exist only to divert funding to or through the hands of the ruling class. Strip these out, and the costs might come substantially down. I would suggest privatisation of all medical services—though paid for by the State, these do not have also to be provided by it—and radical deregulation of all the medical professions: such regulation does not work, and never was intended to work, in the interests of patients.[76]

Here, it is worth a brief mention of the private charities. Conservatives have long regarded these as somehow separate from and superior to the State. This is not presently so. The most prominent charities—Oxfam, the RSPCA, the NSPCC, and so forth—are run and staffed by members or at least clients of the present ruling class. They wrap themselves in the mantle of selflessness while pushing an almost wholly political agenda. As they are private bodies, it might not be advisable to shut them down by direct means. But we should reform the charity laws, so that the only organisations able to claim charitable status would be those unambiguously devoted to feeding soup to tramps and looking after foundlings.

Coming back to state welfare, it would even be in our interests to increase some benefits. Adding up all the cuts suggested above we must easily have about a hundred billion pounds. This would fund a huge tax cut. We could also start paying the old something like the income they used to be promised.

We could, for example, guarantee every pensioner in the country a minimum income of £8,000. Assuming a retired population of five million, and an average subsidy of £3,000 per head, the cost would be £15 billion a year—about the same as is now spent on letting the present ruling class play at improving housing, heritage and the environment. With further spending cuts

---

[76] For a note on the effects of regulation "in the public interest", see Appendix Two.

elsewhere, we could in later years raise the subsidy to £10,000. Even without limiting the right to subsidy to those now over forty, this would not impose a crippling burden.

Most talk of the "pensions timebomb" proceeds on the assumption that the £150 billion now absorbed by the present ruling class is an untouchable first charge on the taxpayers. Raising pensions would be just. It would be widely popular. And it would give millions of already conservative electors good reason to keep voting for us. We could explain that the subsidy was only payable because of our attack on the present ruling class, and that the restoration of that class would mean the ending of the subsidy.

Creating Irreversible Change

A restoration is worth guarding against in the early days. Since I do not imagine killing anyone, not all the members and clients of the now displaced ruling class would be out of work or otherwise neutered. The leading members would retain their personal wealth, their contacts with each other, ordinary access to the media, and control of the main opposition parties. There would also still be modish businessmen like Richard Branson, who might take some while to realise that their interests were no longer served by advancing the interests of a displaced ruling class. These would be watching for any opportunity to overturn us and our revolution. This being so, we should avoid giving them issues to exploit, and we should work to build and consolidate support for our revolution. Nevertheless, I see good automatic reasons why any restoration should become progressively less to be feared.

First, the tax cuts and deregulation that smashing the present ruling class allowed would within five years make England the richest and most powerful country in Europe. I will not bother elaborating on this claim. Any libertarian and most kinds of conservative will take it as read. It is enough to say that, because we have grown up not knowing anything better, it is hard to understand exactly how constrained we presently are. A genuine rolling back of the State would produce a burst of economic growth taking us into a world as different from this one as the worst housing estate in Liverpool is from Surrey. The 20th century would then be seen as the statist nightmare that it was, and the displaced ruling class that did so much to produce that nightmare would be correspondingly rejected.

Second, any attempt at restoring the displaced ruling class would need a big rise in taxes. When the Conservatives abolished the Greater London Council, few voters noticed a fall in their domestic rates. Now it has been substantially re-established by New Labour, I have seen no outrage over the rise in council tax. This is because the changes in tax were small in proportion to the whole.

But the cuts I suggest would let income tax be cut to about 10 per cent, and other taxes be altogether abolished. Refunding the displaced ruling class would mean reversing these cuts. It took a long time for the ruling class to achieve its current position. It needed the excuse of two world wars to increase taxes, and then years of holding high taxes steady as a proportion of an expanding national income. Once cut down, there would be little electoral support for increasing these taxes again.

Third, even if we did lose an election, a restored ruling class would face an administrative mountain before it could re-establish itself. It could repeal all our acts of abolition, but this would no more bring back the abolished institutions than repealing the Government of India Act 1946 could bring back the Raj. The buildings and other assets would have been sold. The more effective workers would have disappeared into other employments.

Above all, the records would have been destroyed. An hour in front of a shredding machine can ruin the work of 20 years; and we would have been feeding these machines day and night. All correspondence, all adjudications and other decisions, all internal memoranda and personnel records—in short, everything that gives effectiveness to a bureaucratic institution—would have irretrievably vanished. The restored ruling class might re-enact the statutes under which, say, English Heritage had operated, but would have nothing more to start with than a name, a bitterly contested grant of the taxpayers' money, and a few dozen filing clerks too useless to have found jobs elsewhere. At the very worst for us, it would take a restored ruling class a generation to get back to the position it now enjoys.

Information: The Health of the Ruling Class

Following from this, I suggest that our government of reaction should stop gathering and publishing official information. We should want no more censuses, or balance of payments statistics, or epidemiological surveys—no more government reports or future projections. Though useful to historians, none of this is essential to the sort of government we should wish to run; and all of it is at least potentially dangerous to that government. Information is the health of the present ruling class. It provides the factual underpinning of its legitimising ideologies.

Much of this information is unproven or untrue—look at the claims about global warming or the harmful effects of passive smoking. Much of the rest is true in the technical sense, but is so selective and deprived of context that it does not qualify as information. Look at the statistics on drinking and driving. The dangers are exaggerated by including accidents that involve drunken pedestrians and passengers; and no comparative figures are gathered on the possibly worse effects of driving while tired or after drinking large amounts of coffee. What we have here is an example of socially constructed knowledge. It looks like neutral fact, but really exists to support some ideological bias: in this case, it exists to support an attack on the alcohol industry and to make the rest of us feel guilty about enjoying the products of that industry.

Such knowledge is collected by government bodies, and then fed to the media *via* fake charities. It is used to create a moral panic about a chosen issue. The politicians then act as if pressured by public opinion into doing something oppressive or stupid or both.

Our first big attack on the present ruling class should destroy most of the really dangerous government bodies, and the formally private bodies that now cluster round them would perish like tapeworms in a dead rat. But we should systematise our attack on official information, and make sure that no more is collected. There will be no law to stop anyone from claiming how many Sikh leather fetishists die from drinking unpasteurised milk, and how this is somehow the fault of capitalism and racism. But he would need to collect his own figures and drum up his own support. Without public funding, and the legitimacy that it tends to confer, he would find himself in much the same position of influence as the man who used to wander round Leicester Square telling us to give up on meat and lustful thoughts.

The object of all this, remember, must be victory—victory against the present ruling class in the shortest possible time. And even before the full achievement of victory, we must be looking to the next stage of the counter-revolution, which is building a new and durable order within which people may live freely again.

SIX: A NEW ORDER OF THINGS

Mildly Utopian Thoughts

I come then to outlining the new order of things that might emerge from our counter-revolution. I must of necessity be vague. The conservative movement is a coalition, agreed only on general principles. Its main constituent parts— traditionalist Tories, classical liberals and libertarians—agree on much, but also disagree on much. Whatever settlement we made would depend on the relative weight at the time of our constituent parts.

There is also the possibility—and the need—that other groups may be recruited into this coalition. The current taxonomy of political debate, of "right" and "left" may have some historical value, and even some social value. But its main present function is to divide opposition to the ruling class. There are religious and sexual and social and ethnic minority groups in this country that are presently seen as clients of the ruling class. But while they enjoy certain privileges at the moment that tie them to the ruling class, there is no reason why they might not be brought to a realisation that a conservative order is much more in their long term interest. We need, therefore, to avoid antagonising these groups in any sense that goes beyond the withdrawal of their formally privileged status.

Moreover, much would depend on external circumstances. What we now regard as serious problems might turn out to be easily managed after the destruction of the present ruling class. Equally, matters that we presently ignore might become pressingly serious. Even so, the outlines of our polity seem clear enough. Much effort would go into restoring as many of our historic institutions as could be saved. It should again be made plain to all of us and to any foreign visitors that this is England, a country quite unlike any other. Politics should be cleaned up, power mostly decentralised; and there should be an almost paranoid concern about the right to peaceful enjoyment of life, liberty and property.

Taxes and the Economy

Our tax policy should be to take as little as possible, and to ensure that this was collected in the least burdensome and intrusive manner. I would like to see the abolition of both income tax and value added tax and their replacement with property taxes. These are simple to assess and collect, and cannot be used to justify the sort of financial inquisition that we now have.

The main argument against levying the majority of taxes on land used to be that the landed interest was both subjectively and objectively in support of an order that preserved a high degree of freedom for nearly everyone. With the destruction of much of that interest, and the co-option of the rest into the new ruling class, that argument no longer applies. Milking people like the Duke of Westminster would be both fiscally convenient and more counter-revolutionary than revolutionary.

For the first few years of our settlement, it would be necessary to keep some of the older taxes to help pay of the welfare state. In time, however, reduced need for this, and higher tax yields from a richer English people, should let us remove the main traces of fiscal rapacity.

Most economic intervention would already have been made impossible by the abolition of the various regulatory bodies. The effect of our changes would be the enabling of a domestic free market. Again, while libertarians would strongly approve of this, many traditionalist Tories might be less happy with the almost complete lack of regulation. Markets can be unruly places, and they often reward the vulgar and unconventional. But this is not primarily a matter of economic justice or efficiency. It is about dismantling structures of power that entrench our present ruling class.

Now, here I will make a clarification for the sake of reaching out to potential allies who do not presently see themselves as part of our conservative movement. There are many people who see themselves as on the "left" of politics, and who also do not like the idea of living in a police state. Some of these people, no doubt, are frauds. I do not believe that most of the people involved in bodies like the National Council for Civil Liberties are serious about freedom. People who believe in an extended state may not approve of its specific acts, but cannot be regarded as potential allies for its destruction.

But there are many anarchists and syndicalists and libertarian socialists who do not believe in this extended state. And so I will make it clear that when I talk about a free market, I do not mean a legal framework within which giant corporations are able to squeeze their suppliers, shut down their small competitors and socialise their workers into human sheep.

I have already said I would not defend the landed interest. I would very strongly favour an attack on the structures of corporate capitalism.

Organisations like Tesco, British Petroleum and ICI are not free market entities. They are joint stock limited liability corporations. The Company Acts allow them to incorporate so that their directors and shareholders can evade their natural responsibilities in contract and tort. They are, for this reason, privileged in law. The alleged justification is that, without such limiting of liability, ordinary people would not invest money in organisations that provide us with necessary or useful products. The institution is, however, undesirable.

It is not true that big business has in any sense suffered from the public interventions in economic activity of the past hundred years. The truth is that big business has benefited from, and in many cases, promoted every agenda of big government. Employment protection laws, product safety laws, curbs on advertising and promotion, heavy taxes, and all the rest—these have served to insulate big business from their smaller competitors, or have cartelised or externalised costs, thereby reducing the need for competition between big business.[77]

The leaders of large corporations are nothing more than the economic wing of the ruling class. They provide taxes and outright bribes that enrich the political wing. They act as part of its ideological state apparatus. Look at the willing compliance of these organisations with every diversity and recycling and anti-smoking law passed. Look at the way in which contracts of work are used

---

[77] There is a large, though mostly American, literature on this point. See, for example, Murray Rothbard: "Every element in the New Deal program: central planning, creation of a network of compulsory cartels for industry and agriculture, inflation and credit expansion, artificial raising of wage rates and promotion of unions within the overall monopoly structure, government regulation and ownership, all this had been anticipated and adumbrated during the previous two decades. And this program, with its privileging of various big business interests at the top of the collectivist heap, was in no sense reminiscent of socialism or leftism; there was nothing smacking of the egalitarian or the proletarian here. No, the kinship of this burgeoning collectivism was not at all with socialism-communism but with fascism, or socialism-of-the-right, a kinship which many big businessmen of the twenties expressed openly in their yearning for abandonment of a quasi-*laissez-faire* system for a collectivism which they could control.... Both left and right have been persistently misled by the notion that intervention by the government is *ipso facto* leftish and antibusiness." (Murray N. Rothbard, "Left and Right: The Prospects for Liberty," *Left & Right* 1, no. 1, Spring 1965.

For further discussions, see: Gabriel S. Kolko, *Railroads and Regulation, 1877-1916*, Princeton University Press, Princeton, 1965 and *The Triumph of Conservatism: A Reinterpretation of American History, 1900-1916*, Free Press, New York, 1965; Murray N. Rothbard, "War Collectivism in World War I" in Ronald Radosh and Murray N. Rothbard, eds., *A New History of Leviathan*, Dutton, New York, 1972; Robert Higgs, *Crisis and Leviathan: Critical Episodes in the Growth of American Government*, Oxford University Press, Oxford and New York, 1987; Paul Weaver, *The Suicidal Corporation: How Big Business Fails America*, Simon & Schuster, New York, 1988; Butler Shaffer, *In Restraint of Trade: The Business Campaign Against Competition, 1918-1938*, Bucknell University Press, Lewisburg, 1997; John T. Flynn, *As We Go Marching*, Free Life, New York, 1973; Roy Childs, *Big Business and the Rise of American Statism*, unnamed publisher, 1971; Joseph Stromberg, "Political Economy of Liberal Corporatism" and "The Role of State Monopoly Capitalism in the American Empire", both from the Center for Libertarian Studies, New York, 1978; Kevin A. Carson, *The Iron Fist Behind the Invisible Hand : Corporate Capitalism as a System of State-Guaranteed Privilege*, Red Lion Press, Montreal, 2001; Kevin A. Carson, *Austrian and Marxist Theories of Monopoly-Capital: A Mutualist Synthesis*, Economic Notes 102, The Libertarian Alliance, London, 2004.

I particularly commend the works of Kevin Carson. See also Appendix Two for a more extended discussion of these matters.

to deter people from engaging in dissident politics. In return for all this, they receive various kinds of protection and subsidy that allow them to make large profits.

They police their workers. But not much overt policing is required. Most policing is through systematic brainwashing. Workers find themselves gently conscripted into large organisations that strip them of autonomy and suppress any actual desire for self-direction. Anyone who works for any length of time in one of these big corporations tends to become just another "human resource"—all his important life decisions made for him by others, and insensibly encouraged into political and cultural passivity. He is essentially a bureaucrat. He knows nothing of how real business is transacted. He cares nothing about laws and taxes that stop others from transacting real business, and so consents to the further expansion of an already bad system.

These organisations do undoubtedly produce things that people want to buy. As such, they are different from the old nationalised utilities. Even so, they are state-privileged trading bodies. They are creatures of the state. Without incorporation, they would have trouble attracting capital from ordinary members of the public. Without incorporation, they would follow the same cycle of growth, flourishing and decline as their human founders. They could not continue from generation to generation, continually renewed by changes of personnel and able to grow ever larger.

If these organisations do produce actual wealth, they are not necessary for its production. I do not believe there would be no extended patterns of commerce without them. There is the financing of ventures by bonds, or their organisation through the voluntary clustering of small businesses. And there is the known tendency of individuals to bring wholly unexpected and elegant solutions to problems when they are free to associate as they please.

Our policy towards these organisations should be to strip them of their protections and subsidies. Free trade should mean no controls on foreign trade. There should be no promotion and underwriting by the State of their domestic or foreign activities. All business costs that are presently externalised should so far as possible be made to fall on those who are naturally responsible for them.

Above all, we should work towards the abolition of limited liability. This is the main legal basis of their existence. Like the political wing of the ruling class, they are enabled by the State, and they can be destroyed by the State. And, looking only at expediency, we should not confine our attack on the present ruling class to just one of its wings.

We should promote the emergence of markets in which the majority of players are sole traders and partnerships and worker cooperatives, and in which the number of people employed on contracts of permanent service is an ever-dwindling minority. This is a moral policy, because it enables a natural order, not requiring positive sustenance by the State. It would be very different from the economic structure we presently have, though probably not less productive of things people wanted to buy. It would replace armies of ruling class serfs with beneficiaries of our counter-revolution.

The matter of how to abolish limited liability requires more discussion than would be appropriate to a book of this length or purpose. But it is worth stating as clearly as I can that, when I talk of free markets, I most certainly do not mean the established models of corporate capitalism.

The Criminal Law

Our criminal law reforms should be largely to clear away the corruptions of the past few generations. I would suggest abolishing all new criminal offences created since around 1960. This would sweep away all the laws against speech and publication made in the name of racial equality, together with a mass of controls on our actions that are unnecessary in themselves and that are enforced only by various kinds of inquisition backed by powers of entry to and search of private property.

As a libertarian, I would go further and repeal all the laws against sale and possession of recreational drugs, and all the laws against the right to keep and use weapons for defence. These are unjust and intrusive laws, and their repeal would be attended by obvious social benefits. However, I will repeat that our movement is a coalition, and not every strand of opinion within it might be happy to see drugs and guns as freely available as they were before 1920. But abolishing all new offences made since 1960 would make guns much easier to acquire, and would make the more objectionable parts of the "war on drugs" impossible.

I will now speak again about the need to reach out to groups not presently in the conservative coalition. There are some traditionalist Tories who dislike homosexuality or any other sexual nonconformity, and would like to reverse the greater social and legal toleration that these nonconformists have enjoyed in the past two generations.

As a libertarian, I would be prepared to start a long and acrimonious opposition to such attempts. It is not the business of the authorities to tell adults how to live—and especially how to behave in private.

Leaving aside principle, however, I would urge caution on pragmatic grounds. Of course, the various "equality" laws that tell hoteliers they must make facilities available for homosexual guests, and so forth, must be repealed. No one should be forced to enable or participate in what he thinks is wrong.

No one should be forced to associate against his conscience. No one has the right to be loved. No one has any right to approval not freely given. As in business, so in other areas, people should be made to live with the consequences of the choices they make and not pass on the costs to others.

But that is all. All else aside, it would be foolish to alienate homosexuals by insisting on prohibitive laws that perhaps the majority of people would agree were immoral—and that were for the most part unenforceable except by the sort of intrusive legislation that required a powerful ruling class.

There is no reason why the majority of homosexuals should ever define themselves as human beings purely by their sexual preferences. All homosexuals pay taxes. Probably most are property owners, and suffer the same regulation of their property rights as everyone else. Many are by nature strongly conservative.[78]

Another pragmatic consideration is that there are some very powerful homosexual networks in this country. They have colonised and cartelised whole sectors of life. The worst effects of such nepotism can be eliminated by the abolition of the various forms of positive and implied support presently given by our extended state. But common preferences will always entail common interests, and perhaps common purpose. Do we really want to stir up opposition that might not otherwise exist? Do we really want to make potential allies, or at best neutrals, into actual enemies?

We should try, therefore, so far as possible to abolish all remaining laws not directed against force or fraud or needed to preserve a narrowly defined national security. This done, we should impose harsh, deterrent penalties for the real crimes that remained. Our new order should not be a safe haven for the enemies of life or property.

This being said, our changes of legal procedure should be directed at restoring all common law protections of the accused. If people are to face very severe punishments, they should first be given every benefit of the doubt.

---

[78] Take this letter from Mark Brown, for example, published in *The Times* on the 30th May 2007: "Sir, As a gay man of 40 years, I feel that Peter Tatchell's representation for gay equality in Russia this weekend was a very foolish move (report, May 29 [*Mr Tatchell had gone to a homosexual march in Moscow and been beaten up by the Russian police*]).

"While I am horrified that he was attacked in this way, what on earth did he think he would achieve by trying to voice his opinion in another country, which clearly has its own values? He certainly did not represent me, or my partner of 24 years.

"I am furious that he thinks he can go anywhere he likes and push the gay rights points across to others. If the Russians want equality, they will have to fight for it themselves."

I know nothing of Mr Brown's general opinions. But he strikes me as a natural conservative, or at least a potential ally. Is there anyone mad enough to want to alienate his support of our counter-revolution?

Perhaps hanging is the just punishment for murder. Perhaps a generation of hard labour is the just punishment for housebreaking. But let it be done with all due process of law.

This means reversing all the changes made since Margaret Thatcher began the present Europeanising of our law. It means restoring the right to silence under police questioning, the full right of *habeas corpus*, the full presumption of innocence, the full right of peremptory challenge of jurors, the rules against similar fact and hearsay evidence, the unanimity rule in jury trials, the double jeopardy rule, and all else that has been taken away.

As a matter of course, all fixed penalties and cautions and the like should be abolished. There should be no punishment except by due process; and there should be at least a great reduction in the number of offences triable by magistrates only. If there are to be fewer criminal offences, the cost argument against jury trials surely falls to the ground.

It might be useful, moreover, to codify the whole of the criminal law, so that all offences and modes of procedure could be set out in a single instrument— and establishing the rule that whatever was not contained in this code could not be regarded as a criminal offence. This would allow people to know exactly how they were constrained in their actions, and make it harder for governments to create new offences without public scrutiny. At the moment, changes to the criminal law are generally made by amending legislation that refers to previous Acts in a manner that requires a law degree and much attention to track. This is unacceptable and should not be allowed to continue.

The Civil Law

Our legal reforms would tend on the civil side to make the law simpler and cheaper and more accessible. There is little more to be said in this area, as the tendency of reform is already in this direction. It is now easier than ever before for ordinary people to conduct their own civil cases, relying on friends and the occasional professional consultation for advice. This is a welcome development.

Our own changes should be to preserve or to restore the traditional forms under which justice has always been done. This means, for example, bringing back names like "writ" and "plaintiff" and "bailiff", and ensuring that Judges and barristers continue to dress in their traditional clothing and observe the traditional courtesies.

The Constitution

We need in general a new constitutional settlement. The one that emerged from the struggles of the 17th century has proved ineffective against the regrowth of despotism in the 20th century. The class interests on which that settlement rested have passed away. Even before the Blair Government began abolishing its external forms, the spirit had departed.

I cannot begin to discuss the details of this settlement. But I suggest it should be based on a written and highly explicit bill of rights. It should also dispense with the Church of England, which has become the spiritual wing of the present ruling class where not simply an object of contempt, and with the House of Lords, which rested before its 1998 reform on no great and respected body of interests, and which is now simply an impediment to the changes we need to make.

The Church should be disestablished and left to wither or reform itself. It should be replaced by a secular state. The House of Lords should be replaced by some kind of Senate. We might call this the House of Lords, and grant life or temporary peerages to its members. But an assembly of landowners has no present legitimacy—nor any probable use to us—and an assembly of political appointees is corrupting.

What of the Monarchy? Should this be retained? On the one hand, our movement should not interfere with historic institutions unless there is compelling need. On the other hand, the Monarchy has been co-opted by the present ruling class as a front organisation. Its function now is to persuade the unreflective that there have been no fundamental changes. The reign of our present Queen has been, so far as I can tell, one long and uncomplaining surrender to the forces of revolution. She seems to have regarded her Coronation Oath as nothing more than a set of quaint words.

There is nothing to be done with the Queen. She is too old to be changed. What of her heirs? Will they join with the present ruling class in defending the existing order of things? Looking at the Prince of Wales and at his children, the answer might be yes. In this case, we might need—bearing in mind the urgency of our counter-revolution—to look at some change in the order of succession, or perhaps even at some kind of republic. But perhaps the next generations of the Monarchy might be brought to remember the terms of the 17th century settlement—that we pretend they are the Lord's Anointed, in return for which they respect our liberties.

There are Tories who will be shocked at this willingness to consider dispensing with still more of the traditional forms than have already gone. But given that the bird is dying, it really is not appropriate to pity the plumage. Tradition is a living force. Traditionalism should not be seen as a blind acceptance of everything inherited from the past. When an institution has outlasted its legitimacy, or when it has been converted to malign ends, it must be either reformed or abolished.

Abolition should not be on grounds of transient or incidental inconvenience. It should certainly not be for reasons of logical tidiness. Wherever possible, ancient forms should be preserved in their outward appearance and adapted to modern uses. After all, one of the main reasons why the Great Revolution failed in France was the wanton abandoning of symbols that restrained the will of men to unbridled power.

But it must always be considered that the Monarchy draws its legitimacy from the support it gives to the forces of conservatism. If it opposes these forces, it becomes just as much an obstacle to reaction as the BBC, and may be dealt with in almost as summary a manner.

In short, the ancient Constitution has broken down, and serious thought must be given to its reconstruction.

The Union

I have referred throughout this manifesto mostly to England. This is because I do not know if the United Kingdom would survive our counter-revolution. It would be nice if it could. Four hundred years of a united Crown, and three hundred of a common Parliament, are not things to be lightly forgotten. But Scotland is ruled far more absolutely than England by the present ruling class, and it lacks the cultural bias to libertarianism that prevents England from becoming a complete police state. Moreover, a significant wing of the present ruling class is made up of Scotchmen in whom ignorance of the English tradition is mingled with hatred of England as a nation. It might, therefore, be convenient to abolish the Union.

If so, the present trend towards separation should be accelerated from London. The Act of Union should be repealed. If the Monarchy is retained in England, the Scotch should be allowed to keep our Monarch as their head of state, thereby placing them in the same position with regard to England as the White Dominions now are.

I will add, for the sake of clarity, that the citizen of no other country should be allowed to vote in English Elections. Nor should these citizens be allowed, without full naturalisation, to stand in English elections.

I see no reason for hard bargaining over money. The Scotch should be allowed to keep whatever revenue can be raised from the oil in their waters as these were determined before the Union. We should keep the whole national debt. We might give *some* preferential treatment to Scottish aliens resident in England, always stopping short of political rights. We should allow trade with Scotland on terms at least as favourable as we allow with other foreign countries.

For Scotland, independence might be more beneficial than its opponents believe. Certainly, a rational English Government would do its best to enable a prosperous and friendly Scotland. With these advantages, it should be quite easy for a prudent Scottish Government to remain solvent and to allow brisk economic growth. A prosperous Scotland is obviously in English interests. And if the Scottish economy should fail, there should be no excuse given to the maniacs who lurk up there closer to the centre than ours do here to cry out that England has ruined their country.

This leaves the problem of what to do with Wales and Ulster. My solution is to force independence on them whether they want it or not. The Ulster Protestants should be given independence—again, whether or not they want it. Of course, they should also be given all they need to defeat the IRA, and should be encouraged to deal justly with their Catholics. But it would not be a problem for England if they decided to opt for the same ethnic and religious cleansing as the Southern Irish carried out after 1922.

Foreign Policy

I have already discussed the European Union. Immediate and total withdrawal is a non-negotiable part of our agenda. But turning to foreign policy in general, we should work towards isolationism. The war in Iraq is now generally accepted to have been a disaster. But so is the war in Afghanistan. So was the war with Serbia. The Cold War and the two world wars served no valuable national interest. We should withdraw from NATO and every other military alliance. We need armed forces sufficient to defend our own territory. We should not pretend that it is either our duty or our ability to join in policing the world.

It is arguable that British power, when it was in the hands of a conservative ruling class, was a force for good in the world. It is hard to argue that now. Since 1945, we have assisted in propping up some of the nastiest governments around that were not formally Marxist-Leninist. Our recent interventions have produced cataracts of blood with no redeeming benefit—either to ourselves or to the people where we have intervened.

This means a break with the United States. There is much talk among American neo-conservatives and their British friends of an "Anglosphere"—that is, of a loose union between the English-speaking peoples to pursue common interests. Whatever this might have been in the time of Cecil Rhodes, it has, since 1945, never amounted to more than a cover for American domination.

The "special relationship" is not, and is not likely in the future to be, in our interest. There might be common interests to pursue if America had a government that operated according to its Constitution. But that country is run by a ruling class similar to our own in its domestic policies, and ruthlessly aggressive in exporting its model of corporatist multiculturalism to other parts of the world. In this respect, it holds a position similar to that of Russia in the Holy Alliance, or between 1945 and 1989.

The American people, I should stress, are in no sense to be regarded as our enemies. They are fellow victims of what—bearing in mind the links between London and Washington—may be seen as almost a single ruling class. They are our fellows in language and culture, and often in blood. Their conservative movement, properly defined, and ours are a single opposition to the single ruling class.[79] But an alliance, after our own counter-revolution, for any purpose with the present ruling class in America is not to be considered.

At first, we might need an understanding with Russia to disappoint what ambitions the European Union and United States still had against our counter-revolution. We might also find ourselves drawn into still more unlikely alliances in defence of our national independence. But these are contingencies that cannot be calculated briefly enough for full discussion here.

I suggest above that we should abolish the Foreign Office. This is partly because it is a citadel of the present ruling class with much status at home and abroad, and because those in it have not noticeably advanced any national interest that I can think of during the past hundred years. Setting up a new Foreign Department, with new structures and new personnel, might deprive us of some useful experience, but would give us a more selfish and therefore rational set of relationships with the rest of the world.

Race and Immigration

I come now to a matter that prudence encourages me to overlook. It is still just about legal in this country to discuss race and immigration. But the lack of criminal sanctions is balanced by informal penalties that may be still more effective at halting discussion.

I believe that the main causes of native discontent on this matter can be removed by the repeal of all anti-discrimination laws and by the restoration of free speech on all issues. People would then be free to live in communities as mixed or as segregated as they wanted, and to say whatever they thought about

---

[79] Here, I will refer to the following books of Paul Gottfried, one of the most prominent American conservatives: *After Liberalism: Mass Democracy in the Managerial State*, Princeton University Press, Princeton, 1999; *The Strange Death of Marxism: The European Left in the New Millennium*, University of Missouri Press, Missouri, 2005. Since I read these only after having written most of this book, I cannot say they influenced me in my own analysis. But the broad similarity of what we are both saying indicates either that I was influenced though some forgotten intermediary, or that we arrived at the same conclusions independently.

the presence here of immigrants and those descended from immigrants.

At the same time, economic freedom is a great social lubricant. It brings people together in forms of cooperation where ethnic origin is far less important than the goods and services they have to offer each other.

I am also dubious about the actual hostility even of Moslems to our way of life. The more I think about it, the more firmly I reject the idea that a conflict is inevitable between Islam and the West. There is a problem in many western countries with large numbers of unassimilated Islamic immigrants. Some of these talk about Islamisation of their host countries and the establishment of a new Caliphate. More practically, the unassimilated have been used by the ruling class as a dissolving force against our own way of life.

But I have more contacts with these people than most of my readers, and I just do not believe their presence here is a critical problem. Burning hatred of our civilisation is not an issue in Oldham and Bradford. Nor was it in the slums of Baghdad before we began strip searching women there and dragging men off the streets into torture chambers.

Islam is not some theological equivalent of Marxist-Leninism. It is an immensely diverse and sophisticated religion. As a classicist, I regret that perhaps two thirds of what used to be the Roman Empire are now within the Islamic world. But Islamic rule for many centuries offered more tolerant and less rapacious government than the Byzantine and mediaeval Catholic states.

Islam is Osama bin Laden. It is also Hassan al-Turabi, and Avicenna, and the Shiite clerics who sat in the first Iranian Parliament in 1906. It is not our enemy unless we try harder than we so far have to make it that.

The real enemy, it must be repeated again and again, is our own ruling class. It is not Moslems in this country who are telling us to be ashamed of our past, and are gutting the museums, and using the schools and media to turn out generations of illiterate sheep. Moslems are not abolishing our ancient freedoms in the name of administrative convenience. It is not Moslems who have bled the old middle classes white with taxes that have then been used to pauperise much of the working class and to raised up a totalitarian clerisy. It is not Moslems who go about insisting that arithmetic is a discourse and the law of contract a set of self-referential artefacts. If our civilisation collapses, it will not be Moslems who have hollowed it out from within.

The real enemy is not dressed in a *jalabiya* or a turban: he wears an Armani business suit, and is fluent in postmodernese. And with the current "war on terror", he is just as hostile to Moslems who want to be left alone as to the rest of us.

This granted, our movement is a coalition. Just as the more conservative need to accept a greater degree of social and economic freedom than they might think desirable, so libertarians must accept a restrictive policy on immigration.

We must, therefore, accept an end to new immigration from outside Europe and the English-speaking world. At the very least, we should require any such immigrants to come in only with security given by existing citizens for their support and good behaviour. As ever, the aim should be to ensure that people bear the whole cost of their actions.

We must stop accepting refugees from other parts of the world, and deport those refugees whose home countries are no longer exceptionally dangerous. The several million illegal immigrants who have been allowed to enter during the past ten years or so must be deported. In those cases where they will not tell where they came from, they must be deported to whatever third world countries can be bribed into accepting them. Zimbabwe is a good possibility here. Sooner or later, Robert Mugabe will drop dead. When this happens, those who replace him will surely be open to any deal that secures them a large and possibly continuing stream of income.

The ethnic minorities remaining should then be treated in exactly the same way as native citizens. We should bring about the third possible outcome mentioned above. There should no recognition of languages other than English and perhaps Welsh; no removal of symbols that might be seen as offensive or "non-inclusive"; no public accommodation of private social or religious differences. So long as there is any education provided by the State, all children should be taught the Indian Mutiny as an uprising of villainous sepoys against "us", and that the abolition of the slave trade and of slavery itself were triumphs of "our" civilisation.

There is no need for intrusion into private arrangements—certainly none for any of the present ruling class suggestion of getting ethnic minorities to wrap themselves in the Union Flag and learn a random set of facts about this country, even if these do not, as at present, amount to ruling class propaganda. Freedom and free institutions have a remarkable capacity for turning strangers into fellow citizens.

But this is no time for arguments in favour of open borders and a state machinery devoid of all historic associations.[80]

---

[80] It is often believed that libertarians are necessarily in favour of open borders, and therefore do not wish to prevent mass immigration. While this is the case with some, it is not the case with all libertarians. Hans-Hermann Hoppe, for instance, stands in the tradition of Ludwig von Mises and Murray Rothbard. He regards the mass immigration of the past half century into western countries as an instance of "forced integration".

He says: "[L]et us…assume an anarcho-capitalist society…..All land is privately owned,

Liberty and Tradition

I think it is worth discussing, however briefly, the institutional arrangements of the new order to which we should be working. But I do not care at all to discuss the private arrangements of this society. Describing the paving stones of Utopia is something best left to the totalitarians.

I do not know how people would choose to live in a really free and wealthy country. They might want to go hunting in the morning and listen to string quartets in the evening, though I doubt this. I suspect that most would rather get married, have children, and stay married, leading lives that intellectuals would consider utterly dull. A few might want to live in free love communes, or play very dangerous sports, or whatever. I can only say is that there would be no government barriers to their living as they pleased—nor any obligation for others to share whatever costs might be involved.

What little I have said in the past few pages might indicate that I am looking to a predominantly libertarian settlement. This is true. But freedom is a large

---

including all streets, rivers, airports, harbors, etc.. With respect to some pieces of land, the property title may be unrestricted; that is, the owner is permitted to do with his property whatever he pleases as long as he does not physically damage the property owned by others. With respect to other territories, the property title may be more or less severely restricted. As is currently the case in some housing developments, the owner may be bound by contractual limitations on what he can do with his property (voluntary zoning), which might include residential vs. commercial use, no buildings more than four stories high, no sale or rent to Jews, Germans, Catholics, homosexuals, Haitians, families with or without children, or smokers, for example.

"Clearly, under this scenario there exists no such thing as freedom of immigration. Rather, there exists the freedom of many independent private property owners to admit or exclude others from their own property in accordance with their own unrestricted or restricted property titles. Admission to some territories might be easy, while to others it might be nearly impossible. In any case, however, admission to the property of the admitting person does not imply a 'freedom to move around,' unless other property owners consent to such movements. There will be as much immigration or non-immigration, inclusivity or exclusivity, desegregation or segregation, non-discrimination or discrimination based on racial, ethnic, linguistic, religious, cultural or whatever other grounds as individual owners or associations of individual owners allow.

"Note that none of this, not even the most exclusive form of segregationism, has anything to do with a rejection of free trade and the adoption of protectionism. From the fact that one does not want to associate with or live in the neighborhood of Blacks, Turks, Catholics or Hindus, etc., it does not follow that one does not want to trade with them from a distance. To the contrary, it is precisely the absolute voluntariness of human association and separation—the absence of any form of forced integration—that makes peaceful relationships—free trade—between culturally, racially, ethnically, or religiously distinct people possible. (Hans-Hermann Hoppe, *On Free Immigration and Forced Integration*, 1999—available at: *http://www.lewrockwell.com/orig/hermann-hoppe1.html* (checked June 2007))

part of the English tradition. If our tradition involved things like slavery, female circumcision and a rigid caste system, the settlement I am imagining would have no support from conservatives. But, of course, the English tradition is about things like equality before the law, trial by jury, freedom of the press, and the pursuit of commercial advantage.

Traditionalist Tories may not agree with everything that libertarians believe, but the institutions they want to preserve are broadly libertarian. Moreover, even if a powerful state run by them might do more to preserve tradition than my recommended system of semi-*laissez-faire*, such a state is not currently on offer. For at least the foreseeable future, a powerful state in England must be run by the present ruling class. At least free men only reject traditions that have ceased to be useful, and the rest survive.

As for my fellow libertarians, I suggest that liberty can only survive for any time when embodied in conservative institutions. Though large, the benefits of liberty are often less visible than its inconveniences. For every one person who can argue the case for trial by jury on its merits, there may be hundreds who are against abolishing it simply because it has always existed. Libertarians, then, are well-advised to pay some respect to traditions and institutions in a country like England that do not in themselves seem to be libertarian. They are all part of the same web that holds us to the past.

There may come a time when libertarians and traditionalist Tories will find themselves seriously divided. Then the conservative movement will splinter. But for the moment, we are natural allies against a ruling class that is at war with both liberty and tradition.

Never mind the strong historic links that hold us within a single movement. We live in an age when conservatives must be libertarian and libertarians conservative.

SEVEN: FEASIBLITY OF COUNTER-REVOLUTION

Technical Feasibility

There is no doubt that, resolutely carried through, a frontal attack could work. Socialist revolutions have the advantage over our counter-revolution of raising up an administrative class that unambiguously benefits from the changes, and that can be trusted to fight any attempt at reaction. This advantage, however, is largely offset by the failure of this class to achieve any of its stated objectives. Taking over the production and delivery of bread is no easy matter; and socialist revolutions always hit crisis when the shops sell out and there is nothing more to put in them. That is when the killing usually starts.

What is here suggested has none of these disadvantages. The State would simply no longer do things that could be done better through voluntary effort or that should not be done at all. As for the jobs, these would not be missed. There are not enough conservatives with the necessary skills and inclinations to take them on.

We also know that such frontal attacks do work. Our own history gives at least two examples.

From the time of Henry II, English governments found themselves in almost permanent dispute with the Roman Church over its desire to maintain a state within a state. On the whole, the Church won these disputes. Its functions were considered necessary, and only it could perform them. Starting with Thomas Beckett, the tendency of those appointed from outside to govern it was to be absorbed into its own cultural environment. The Church had wealth and status and an entrenched body of intellectual defenders.

The dispute was ended by Henry VIII, who destroyed the Roman Church in England at almost one stroke. He seized its wealth, raise up a new class enriched by the spoliation, and centralised what remained as a much reduced national church under his own control. The reaction under Mary was frustrated not only by her early death, but by her inability to undo the seizure of wealth. And the reaction was easily undone by Elizabeth, who completed the revolution.

The strategy worked again in 1641. The Tudors had created a crude but effective bureaucracy through which they could rule England. This was nothing compared with the administrative growth taking place over much of Western Europe, but it enabled them to set aside large parts of the ancient constitution. By abolishing the administrative councils, the Long Parliament destroyed an entire class of civil lawyers and administrators that would otherwise have checked the rebirth of English liberty.

Though efforts were made in the 1680s to recreate this class, the personnel no longer existed—nor the means to train them. The result was an administrative vacuum which lasted well into the 19th century, and in which the classical age of English civilisation was contained.[81]

The Constitutional Ease of an English Counter-Revolution

This could be repeated in England without any breach of constitutional norms. We have an advantage that other countries have not. In the United States, for example, there is a Federal Government in Washington, 52 State Governments, and hundreds or thousands of local governments. There is also the Supreme Court. The American Constitution was designed by men who wanted to limit power by dividing it. The problem is that the American equivalent of our ruling class have progressively captured every branch and division of government. An American counter-revolution might not require the recapture of every branch and division of government. But American conservatives would need to win dozens of elections, not all of them held in the same year, and then to keep winning them during their counter-revolution.

This is not so in England. There are presently 646 Members of the House of Commons, including the Speaker and his Deputies. Therefore, the conservative movement in Britain needs to win a minimum of 324 seats in the Commons. Given a majority in the House of Commons, we could use the full historic and recent facts of parliamentary supremacy to do whatever we wanted during five years.

Parliament is supreme. It possesses, said A.V. Dicey, "the right to make or unmake any law whatever; and...no person or body is recognised by the law of England as having a right to override or set aside the legislation of Parliament".[82] It could put a man to death today for having done yesterday what was not illegal. It could repeal the Act giving India Independence and appoint a new Viceroy. It could enact that the square of the hypotenuse was not equal to the square of other two sides combined. These laws would all be accepted as binding in the British courts. How these second two might be enforced is unimportant. What is important is that the will of Parliament cannot be formally checked by any other institution in this country. There is no division of powers. There are no autonomous intermediary powers.

There might be a problem with the House of Lords and Monarchy. But these have insufficient legitimacy to frustrate the clearly expressed will of the

---

[81] For a longer discussion of these points, see Sean Gabb, *How English Liberty Was Created by Accident and Custom, and then Destroyed by Liberals*, Historical Notes 31, the Libertarian Alliance, London, 1998.

[82] A.V. Dicey, *The Law of the Constitution* (1885), Macmillan, London, 8th ed 1915, p 38

Commons. Give us a majority in the Commons and we could legally shut down whole areas of the State and remodel the rest to our advantage.

Conservatives have for generations been terrified at the thought of absolute legislative sovereignty. But it exists. It has so far been used as a weapon against us. It is, however, formally possible for us to take control of the weapon and use it against our class enemy.

Present Impossibility

But formal possibility is not the same as actual possibility. The idea that we can, at the moment, get one good conservative elected to Parliament—let alone another 323 or more—is still more bizarre than the plan that some of my friends have been projecting these past thirty years to take over the Conservative Party.

It is worth considering how few reliable people we need in this country to win. At the same time, we must recognise the political and institutional facts that prevent us from getting these people into the right positions.

Anyone who thinks the time is now right for starting a new political party is at least mad. We have a ruling class media supporting ruling class parties. We have an electorate brainwashed by the ruling class media and educational and administrative establishments into voting for the ruling class parties. It is currently impossible to break into this closed political circle. Every attempt at entryism into the main parties has been detected and frustrated. Apparently successful entrants have been co-opted into the ruling class.

As for a new political party, we have had two main warning examples in the past decade. There was the Referendum Party set up by James Goldsmith. I was told by Chris Tame before he died that this party and its election campaign cost £24 million. Not a single candidate was elected. Nearly all lost their deposits.

There is the United Kingdom Independence Party. This does win elections, at least to the European Parliament. But anyone who knows UKIP will know that this party wins elections not because of its personnel and organisation but in spite of them. It is racked by personal and factional hatreds. There are allegations of financial fraud and of security service infiltration. When I see how discussion of the party is turned on in the media for some elections and off for others, I begin to accept the conspiracy theory that it is kept in being only as a means of drawing off support for the more effective—but horribly tainted—British National Party.

Otherwise, there is the fact that our movement is a coalition. We may be agreed on what we do not like. We are not agreed on the details of what we want. If you have disagreed with any of my positive suggestions given above, I ask you to imagine how the pair of us could work harmoniously together on a committee to draw up a party manifesto. And this is without my proposed strategy of reaching out to other groups not presently seen as part of the conservative movement.

I sometimes like to begin monlogues with the words "when I come to power as the front man for a military *coup*...". This allows me to play an enjoyable mental game, but is not a credible substitute for political organisation. A *coup* of the sort described above cannot be attempted in this country without some democratic authority. Governments require more than legal authority. Unless highly despotic, they require more even than the consent of those enforcing their commands. Without a vague sense of legitimacy derived from public opinion, it would be hard for any of us to launch a counter-revolution straight on coming into office.

Besides, no army officer I have met has ever struck me as particularly Cromwellian.

We are thrown back, therefore, on an unwelcome use of the political imagination. For centuries, English political activity has been focussed on Parliament. Every movement for change has concentrated on getting its spokesmen elected to Parliament and at least to influence the Government through the electoral process. This is now closed to us. The Conservative Party is a shambolic fraud. The small parties that many hope will replace it are too badly organised to gather more than the occasional protest vote. If there is to be a final victory for our movement, it must involve a parliamentary majority. But that is a distant prospect. In the meantime, what is to be done?

Clearing Away the Rubbish

My answer in the short term is that we must assist in the destruction of the Conservative Party. While it remains in being as a potential vehicle of government, every initiative from our movement will be taken over and neutralised. We should *never*, in any election, vote for Conservative Party candidates. We should vote for alternative parties, however useless or generally bad they might be. We might even consider voting for other ruling class parties if that were the best means of keeping Mr Cameron and his Quisling Rightists out of office. Or we might not bother voting at all. Abstention may sometimes be as good as a vote—especially if we can make it clear enough that we are abstaining because there is no one to vote for.

This is advice, I grant, that many will reject as unrealistic. The Conservatives will not deliver our counter-revolution or anything like it. They are, however, making credible offers of amelioration. Without promising to overturn the established order of things, they are promising less damaging levels of tax and regulation, and a return to cabinet government and parliamentary and local accountability; and they are promising at least to slow the attack on our civil liberties.

It may be that all the main parties are a ruling class cartel. But the cartel extends only to the overall settlement. There may be significant differences of approach between these parties that makes it worth voting for the Conservatives. They are promising to be less corrupt and oppressive than Labour has been. Bearing in mind just how corrupt and oppressive the present Ministers have been, it would be hard to break this promise.

My response is to ask at what cost amelioration is to be. A Conservative Government would in some respects be better than the one we have or are about to get. Ultimately, though, so what? The Conservatives under Mr Cameron have repeatedly said they have no interest in making fundamental changes. There is no reason to disbelieve this. At the end of five years of Conservative government, therefore, there would have been much political excitement and much appearance that something was being done. But there would, at the end, be still fewer of our historic liberties and still less of our national identity. Except it was more decorous, the transformation of our country would have moved forward as if Labour had never left off ice.

Why then vote Conservative? For myself—and for increasingly many of my friends—if I must be destroyed, let me be speared in the front by someone who looks me in the eye and calls himself my enemy. Far better this than be garrotted from behind by a supposed friend.

In the longer term, we must learn to keep our nerve. Unless we have another of those strokes of luck that have always got us out of trouble in the past, there is no immediate prospect of victory. The present ruling class has too strong an ideological and repressive state apparatus for it to be defeated by simple electoral means. We need to consider a Fabian strategy.

I do not wholly mean by this copying the socialist intellectuals who surrounded the Webbs a hundred years ago. What I have in mind is Quintus Fabius Maximus, who was appointed Dictator during the Second Punic War. Under Hannibal, the Carthaginians had broken into Italy. They had annihilated every Roman army sent against them. As an army in the field, they were unbeatable. And so Fabius avoided battle and let them wear themselves out. Where possible, he harried them with small skirmishes. Otherwise, his main victories were clever retreats that kept his own army in being. Though his strategy was at first unpopular with the more straightforward Romans, he prepared the way for the great victories of Scipio Africanus; and he died the acknowledged saviour of his country. *Unus homo nobis cunctando restituit rem*, said Ennius of him.

Or, again to use the neo-Marxist terminology, we must prepare for a long struggle.

Long Struggle

That is our only available strategy. Elections cost money. They absorb huge amounts of time and effort. Every failure is disheartening. We cannot afford the luxury of thinking we can vote our way to safety. We need instead to create our own media to get our message across. We need to continue organising among ourselves. We need, where appropriate, to use the courts. These are not necessarily expensive. The Internet has transformed the balance of power between the public and the established media.

So long as we can stop tearing each other apart in various internal disputes—the Conservative and UKIP activists are increasingly tiresome in this respect—we already have a large network of publicists. At least two court actions in recent years—over compulsory metrication and the hunting ban—have been successful. They did not achieve their stated aims, but gave the Judges an excuse to change the Constitution in our favour. Though not cheap, they were not prohibitively expensive.

I know that this strategy will be often depressing. It will also be dangerous. I was in a television studio on the evening when Nick Griffin of the British National Party was partially acquitted of offences that should not exist in a free country. I was warned not to discuss his case once the BBC had announced—prior to any decision by the prosecuting authorities—that he would be retried for those offences on which the jury had not been able to reach a verdict.

His party—whatever we may think of it—has been targeted for destruction. Its known members cannot get jobs in the public sector and in growing areas of the private sector. It cannot get its website hosted in this country, and must get its magazine published by an Arab-owned company that has so far been outside the reach of the present ruling class.

Can we assume that these measures will not be extended to us? I am told that, already, applicants for jobs in the Foreign Office are asked if they are or ever have been members of a "Eurosceptic organisation".

Fighting our present ruling class will not be the same as fighting the Attlee, Wilson and Callaghan Governments.

And if victory ever does come, it will be in a transformed country. We shall be like the aristocrats who returned to France in 1814—though ours will have been a mostly liberal reaction. All that we knew and loved in our youths will have been swept away. Much might be recoverable. More will need to be begun over again. The old organic Constitution may have passed beyond recovery, and we shall need to devise some new set of arrangements within which we can recreate the spirit of our past without even what now remain its most hallowed forms.

Though not currently possible, it may one day be possible to destroy the institutional networks through which the ruling class maintains control. However long it may last, and however secure at any one moment, hegemony is never permanently achieved. It can be changed or altogether destroyed by a crisis. More often, it changes with the general climate of ideas within the intellectual classes.

The present ruling class came to power not all at once, but by a silent capture, over several decades, of the main cultural and administrative institutions. We may not by the same means be able to dislodge it from this power. But we can bring forward the moment when the ruling class will eventually run out of commitment, and begins to transform itself into an increasingly timid *ancien régime*. Remember, these people are at war not just with us, but with reality itself. That war must always be lost in the end.

Yes, there are problems with this option. The new ruling class is far less tolerant than the old of dissent, and is far more willing and able to defend its position from the sort of attack that it once made. And we may not have the time for a slow recapture of hegemony. In the long run, we may be dead. Long before then, we may be hopelessly enslaved. But, given that a frontal attack seems not currently to be possible, we have no choice but to settle down to a long struggle.

How to Fight the Battle

If the object is to reverse a cultural revolution, the means must be to wage a cultural war. We need, by a series of countless small strokes, to strip the ruling class of the legitimacy that gives it confidence to act, and that ensures its actions are accepted by the ruled. If we cannot overturn the present order of things, we must content ourselves with sapping its foundations.

The first procedural difficulty with raising any protest at this cultural revolution is that there has been no systematic attempt at collection and analysis of the necessary evidence. By its nature, such evidence is ephemeral—sometimes almost invisible. A plotline or comment in a television soap can be seized on. But the context is which is has meaning cannot be shown, and so the protest tends to look silly. And the next time a protest is made, the earlier occasion has usually slipped from easy recollection.

This attack is not a frontal assault, the nature of which can be seen all at once. It is, much rather, a slow attrition, no one part of which in itself is of any discernable consequence. Nor is the language of protest generally known to those inclined to protest: it is too often locked away in heavy books with long titles and filled with frequently impenetrable jargon.

We need people to collect and analyse the evidence of what is happening, and to make this available. The National Viewers and Listeners Association used to do this for violent and sexually explicit content in the broadcast media—though it did this for the most part very badly, bringing even its methods into disrepute. But there is no one at present to do this for the political content in the media.

Pro-Conservative policy institutes, such as the Adam Smith Institute, the Institute of Economic Affairs, and the Institute of Directors, concentrate on economic issues. Other institutes like Civitas, concentrate mainly on the reform of health and welfare provision. Then there is the Libertarian Alliance, which specialises in producing long-range propaganda for the return to a cultural and economic hegemony of freedom. These are necessary for spreading conservative ideas, but are by no means sufficient.

I once believed in the need for a formal institute that would watch and record and dissect the whole range of popular entertainment in the broadcast media; that would watch and record and dissect biassed reporting in the news media; and that would produce long "deconstructions" of biassed news articles in the manner pioneered by Barry Krusch; and that would pay careful attention to imposed changes in the use or meaning of words. I believed this institute would be useful for taking over the tools of destructive analysis developed by the radical socialists, and turn them against the radical socialist ideological hegemony now being imposed throughout the English-speaking world.

Its overall aim would not have been to produce changes in the law and administration that could be directly traced back to its activities—in the way that many of the Thatcher reforms of the 1980s could be traced back to the Adam Smith Institute or the Institute of Economic Affairs. Rather, it would have been to foster what the Marxists call a "revolutionary consciousness"—that is, to give words to otherwise unnamed ideas in the minds of the ruled, and to expose and thereby delegitimise the agenda of the ruling class.

Perhaps such an institute would be a good idea. However, when I did suggest one, nobody would give me any money; and I now doubt if I am the right man to run it. Fortunately, while it might be desirable, it is no longer necessary. During the past few years, hundreds of broadly conservative blogs have emerged in this country. The majority never do very much, and soon die. But there is a large and growing number of committed bloggers. To these must be added the growing number of radio and television stations that operate *via* the Internet. A whole new alternative media is emerging.

Since I do what I do, and do not welcome close advice on what else I should do, I will not presume to tell others in the alternative media what their duty should be. But I will offer some advice to any person or persons who may feel inclined to take it.

He might care to analyse the plotlines of the television and radio soaps and classify the various techniques of propaganda used, and relate these to each other—always supplying full evidence. This would be made available to anyone who wanted it for whatever use might be desired.

He might further try predicting the resolution of plotlines in these soaps, doing so as part of the exposure of their political agenda. This could be done by parodying the scripts. Or he might offer small prizes to his readers for who could most accurately predict the politically correct resolution of a plotline.

In the case of the broadcast news media, coverage of certain public events could be monitored—with attention given to words used, to spoken emphases, to the order of interviews and contrasting treatment of interviewees, to the length of items, and to the length and order of accompanying items in the broadcast.

For the print media, articles and news stories could be analysed and explained. One way of doing this is by deep linking to the relevant websites. For example, a set of web frames could be created, one of which called up an article by Polly Toynbee from *The Guardian* website, and the other one of which contained a running commentary. This technique was used with great success by the vegetarians who were sued by the McDonald's burger chain in the late 1990s.

These activities might be so far as possible ignored by the ruling class media. would the BBC give much serious attention to people arguing that it was a propaganda tool of a movement dedicated to the overthrow of the established order? Possibly not.

Then again, I have been saying this for years, and am always in demand on the wireless—even if my appearances are normally confined to things like *Drivetime* on Radio Slough. We are not facing a monolith like the Soviet State. Let someone be sufficiently articulate and entertaining, and the ruling class media may be tempted to pay attention.

Spoiling the Egyptians

Then there is the use of formal complaints procedures against the ruling class media. For the most part, the various regulatory bodies are not intended to regulate, but to serve the same decorative or sedative function of courts of law in the old Communist states. But they can be made to serve a valuable purpose. Once evidence had been gathered in sufficient quantity, complaints of bias could be made to the Broadcasting Standards Commission. These could be made as often as offence was taken.

Indeed, once a network of committed activists could emerge across the country, there could be multiple complaints. These complaints might be rejected. If so, exposing the biassed nature of the regulatory bodies could be added to the agenda of some blogger. If successful, their success could be added to the charges against the broadcasters.

In any event, once a formal complaint is made, those complained about are required to spend time of defending themselves. A sufficient number of complaints could make so much work that broadcasters might start, as a matter of economic prudence, to consider some attempt at objectivity.

Where insufficient grounds existed for a formal complaint, activists might complain directly to broadcasters. At the least, this would cause embarrassment. There is no shortage of anger and resentment at the activities of the broadcast and published media.

Concluding Remarks about Money

The advantage of decentralised activism *via* the Internet is that it already exists, if not always focussed on what may be thought the right objects. It also involves little cost. I have been using the Internet for over a decade, and my total direct Internet costs throughout have been under £3,000. I have friends who have managed at much lower cost.

But money must always be an issue. Nearly all of us need to work for a living. Most of us have families to support and with which we want to spend some time before we die. We have worked in some cases for years without external financial support. We have achieved much, given the lack of resources. But much more could be achieved if there were some financial support.

And we shall need more than the decentralised Internet carping that I have just explained. We need the means for proper research and publication. My present analysis, and others like it, are not the last word on the dangers we face. There is much more to be said, and perhaps better said, by others who are scholars as well as polemicists.

We need to run lectures and seminars to promote our ideas to a new generation. We need to hold conferences and debates, so that the various parts of our movement can grow and organise within themselves, and so that they can explore with each other what they have in common and where they must continue to disagree.

All this needs money. And we have none. Money cannot produce a movement that has no intellectual basis. The large sums spent over the years—and wasted—to produce a "force for the radical centre" show the truth of this. Neither though can a movement, even with an intellectual basis, grow properly without money.

And so I will appeal for funding. I appeal for funding for me and for the Libertarian Alliance, and for all the other individuals and groups who make up the conservative movement. I will appeal even for persons and groups who are not on friendly terms with the Libertarian Alliance, but who are undoubtedly part of our movement.

Have you enjoyed reading this book? Has it in any sense enlightened and inspired you? Would you like to see more of the same? If not, I commend your diligence in reading the past 35,000 words, but have nothing more to say to you. If yes, why not send me some money? I have written this book mostly on railway journeys to work—in time that I might more healthily have spent sleeping. Virtually everything I write on politics is done for free. If you really want to encourage me to write more, you should consider following the advice on donation given at the end of this book.

I have written this book with England in mind. But that does not at all prevent me from asking Americans and other foreigners for money. Bearing in mind what I have said about the technical ease by which power in this country might be captured and used, I suggest that the culture war for your own country might be just as effectively won in England as at home.

In asking for money, I assume that you are on a middling to good income, and can spare the occasional small gift. If you fall below that happy position, please keep your money for yourself. If you are already doing something within our movement, again, please keep your money for your own efforts.

But supposing you are rich: supposing I have managed to send this book to someone of real means who has read it this far—what do I want of you?

The short answer is that I want a large sum of money. I want you to give money to me and to all my friends and my various actual and potential allies. I want money to pay for all the things we currently cannot afford, and money to make us feel better about ourselves and our mission.

Please do not waste our time by setting up an institute of your own, funded for one year at a time, and then make little grants to us that are tied to specific tasks. If you are serious about more than making a noise with your wallet that you cannot make with your pen, give money directly, and give or promise money for several years in advance.

Why should you believe your money will not be taken and spent by idlers and charlatans? My answer is that you should try exercising some judgement of character. But it is important that money should be given or promised long term.

We in the conservative movement do not share the good fortune of ruling class intellectuals. There is no dense network for us of charities and companies and government bodies and universities and policy institutes to move between. If funding for these people does come ultimately *via* a single tap that can be turned off, it is diffracted through a shower head with hundreds of individual jets. A ruling class intellectual has no shortage of potential employers, some of which are even at war with each other. That means security for a diverse range of opinions within the ruling class.

We, on the other hand, are generally expressing unfashionable, and sometimes even dangerous, opinions. Because of this, there is a general shortage of opportunities for getting an income. The more outspoken we are, the greater the shortage of opportunities. Short term funding is unlikely to give any of us the security for being as effective as we might be.

If you insist on behaving like certain other "benefactors" of our movement, you will not be advancing our cause. If you hand out little dribbles of money that might stop at any moment, you will become an object of endless sycophantic praise. But you will not ultimately be giving any of us the confidence to do what we need to.

Therefore, give. Give widely. Give generously. Give trustingly. If you will, give anonymously. By all means, think hard before you give about the character of those asking for your money. But, that being done, just give.

To conclude, whatever our means, whatever our views, we need to come together and discuss our vision of an England for the 21st century that is not a gigantic prison camp run by and for our present ruling class. As my contribution to this discussion, I offer my analysis of our common enemy and of how that common enemy may eventually be defeated. Before we can change the world, we need to understand it.

I also offer my suggestion that the conservatism of this century is not to be defined as a living in a country where everyone sits down to a dinner of meat and two vegetables while listening to Max Bygraves records—unless, that is, he wants to. This is a definition cleverly imposed by the ruling class and accepted by both traditionalists and modernisers in the Conservative Party. That is why debate in that Party has settled into a sterile dispute between those who want an agenda of authoritarianism and those who want one of imitative political correctness.

We have lost the battle for our country. This does not necessarily mean we have lost the war. There is a chance—however remote—that we can overturn the existing order of things. All we must do is genuinely want to be a free people again, living in an independent country. On this definition, our allies can be everywhere. They can have nipple rings or green hair. They can be homosexuals or transsexuals or drug users. They can want to live in racially exclusive enclaves. They can be Catholics or Moslems or atheists. Whoever wants to be left alone in his own life, and whoever wants this country to be governed from within this country, is a conservative for the present century.

Whoever will raise a finger towards this object I will count among my friends.

APPENDIX ONE: THE CONSERVATIVE FRAUD

On Fraternity:
Politics Beyond Liberty and Equality
Danny Kruger
Civitas, London, 2007, 95pp, £7.50 (pbk)
ISBN 978 1 903386 57 6[83]

At the beginning of the short book, its author insists that "I do not speak for the Conservative Party". This being said, Dr Kruger is a special adviser to David Cameron and is a former leader writer for *The Daily Telegraph*. He also showed the manuscript of his book to David Willetts, Oliver Letwin, Daniel Hannan, and to various other people more or less closely connected with the Leader of the Conservative Party. It was, moreover, discussed before publication at one of the lunchtime seminars hosted by Civitas. I have attended several of these, and it is easy to imagine that this one was attended by just about every important academic or intellectual connected with the Conservative Party.

The disclaimer, therefore, is a matter of form. The book is—and is intended to be regarded as—an authoritative statement of Conservative Party thought. I do not see how there can be any reasonable doubt of this. But it is a point that I must ask my readers to bear continually in mind. I once sat next to Dr Kruger at a private dinner party. I do not recall that we disagreed on anything. He wrote a very nice article last year, regretting the death of Chris Tame. Some of the names given in his Acknowledgements are of friends. If I now say that this book is an intellectual fraud in its intention, and shabby in its execution, I hope he and they and you will not take my comments as personal.

So far as I can understand him, Dr Kruger is trying to analyse the current state of affairs in this country. During the second half of the 20th century, he says, we tried two great experiments. The first was socialist equality. This began to break down in the 1960s, when trade union privilege and heavy spending on welfare led to inflation and a loss of competitiveness.

The second was a return to market liberty under Margaret Thatcher. This restored the economy, but led to a collapse of various customs and institutions that gave meaning to the lives of individuals. Before coming to power in 1997, Tony Blair did promise to sort out the resulting disorder and general loss of

---

[83] First published as Sean Gabb, *The Emperor Has no Clothes*, Free Life Commentary No.158, 31st March 2007—available on-line at
http://www.seangabb.co.uk/flcomm/flc158.htm

faith in the system. However, since then, that promise has been comprehensively broken. We therefore need a new government that will reconcile the jointly necessary but often opposed impulses of liberty and equality. Thus the title of the book.

Exactly how these impulses are to be reconciled within a new and stable order is not made clear. But Dr Kruger does excuse himself in advance with the statement:

> In this essay I try to outline the political philosophy which justifies the 'communal [but] not official'. It is necessarily abstract, a 'resort to theories', in Burke's disparaging aside. It is devoid of detailed policy, yet I hope it demonstrates that, all our common rhetoric notwithstanding, there are real differences between Right and Left, founded on very different ideas of how society works.[p.11]

This is a wise excuse, as it saves Dr Kruger from having to admit the fraudulent nature of his analysis. For there was no return to market liberty in the 1980s. If it took me until nearly the end of the decade to shake off the false assumptions I had made as a teenager, I was one of the earliest conservatives to understand the real nature of the Thatcher project. It was to reconcile the fact of an extended and meddling state apparatus, plus big business privilege, with the need to generate enough wealth to pay for it all.

There was no reduction in tax for the middle classes. There was no overall cutting of regulations. Instead, the taxes and regulations were revised so that we could, by immense hard work, reverse the long term relative decline of the British economy.

As for the working classes, their ability to slow the growth of gross domestic product was checked by the ending of various—and perhaps indefensible—protections, and by the importation of a new proletariat from elsewhere in the world that had no perceived commonality of interest with the native working classes, and that would, by its presence, drive down their living standards.

So much for economic liberty. Where other liberties were concerned, we saw a consistent rolling back of the gains made since about 1600. Procedural safeguards were shredded, so that the law was turned from a shield for the people into a sword for the state. A close surveillance was imposed over our financial affairs. Freedom of speech and association were eroded—partly by direct changes in the law, partly by creating a general environment within which disobedience to the expressed will of the authorities became unwise. At the same time, verbal and institutional associations that bound us to a more liberal past were progressively broken; and structures of democratic accountability were replaced by indirect rule from Brussels and from a more general New World Order.

The election of a New Labour Government changed very little. Government under Tony Blair became more politically correct than it would have been under the Conservatives. But this was balanced by a greater caution in matters of European harmonisation. The destruction of the Common Law and its replacement by a panopticon police state went on regardless.

There is not—and has not been during the past quarter century—any political conflict in this country between liberty and equality. We are both less equal today than we were in about 1980, and we are less free. Such debate as there is between the two main political parties is over details. The project common to both Labour and Conservative Parties is the transformation of this country into a place where the upper reaches of the ruling class can enjoy a status and relative wealth not known since early Stuart times—and in which there can be no challenge from below.

The Conservatives under Mrs Thatcher started this. It was continued by Labour under Mr Blair. It will not be reversed by the Conservatives under Mr Cameron.

Given these facts, it is not surprising that Dr Kruger has refused to discuss any detailed policies. Where nothing new is intended, nothing at all should be promised.

But this brings me to the apparent purpose of the book. Our politics may be degraded from the level even of the late 1970s. But we have yet to sink entirely to the level of America, where elections seem to be decided wholly by money and competing armies of drum majorettes. It is still expected that political debate in this country should proceed from an intellectual basis. The Conservatives have no intellectual basis that they dare honestly explain to us. They must at the same time convey the impression of one. They have, therefore, put Dr Kruger up to write a whole book about Conservative principle, but to do so in a way that will allow almost no one to understand him.

The language of his book is in all matters of importance pretentious and obscure.

Take, for example, this:

> Central to the Hegelian concept of *Aufhebung* or 'sublation' is the preservation of the antithetic stages passed through by the thesis. Not only is the thesis 'realised' by its sublation: the antithesis too is strengthened and perpetuated. But the thesis only preserves those elements of the antithesis it finds conducive to itself—there must be, in the key Hegelian word, an 'ethical' relationship between thesis and antithesis, by which one relates to another in a natural and organic manner.[p.18]

Or take this:

> The person abstracted from all contingent circumstances—the main in isolation—is not truly a man at all, merely (Hegel again) 'the sheer *empty unit* of the person'. The original Kantian individual who signs the social contract from behind the veil of ignorance, with his objective intellect and dispassionate morality, is admirable and necessary. But he is not enough.[p.49]

Or take this:

> For freedom is attained, said Hegel, not by the individual divorcing himself from society but by marrying it. True—what he called 'concrete'—freedom is not 'the freedom of the void'. It is the freedom of 'finding oneself' in society; of 'being with oneself in another'. By my marriage with society I attain my true self, which before was abstract. I am realised, socialised; I whisk aside the veil of ignorance, 'the colourful canvass of the world is before me'; I plunge into it, and find myself 'at home'.[p.51]

The meaning of this second and third can perhaps be recovered. They appear to mean that individuals function best when they are surrounded by familiar things that give meaning and security to their lives. As to the first, your guess is as good as mine.

There is page after page of this stuff. We have commonplaces dressed up to look profound. We have manifest nonsense. We have knowing references to Plato and Aristotle and Hobbes and Burke and Mill. We have untranslated words and phrases, or words that have been taken into English but never widely used. There is, of course, "*Aufhebung*". This is at least translated—though, until I looked it up in a dictionary, I could only understand "sublation" from its Latin roots. But there is also "noumenal"[p.13], "heteronomous"[p.38], "*soixantes-huitards*"[p.40], "thetic"[p.66], and much else besides. Oh—and we have the word "discombobulated"[p.58]. This is an illiterate Americanism from the 1830s, and has no fixed meaning. Such meaning as Dr Kruger gives it must be gathered from the context in which he uses it.

There are many subjects, I grant, discussion of which requires a specialised language. There is music. There is the law. There are the natural sciences. But this is so only for the most elaborate discussions. For basic presentations, plain English has always been found sufficient. And it is not so for discussing political philosophy. For this, plain English is ideally suited. I do know languages—Slovak, for example—where foreign or unfamiliar words are needed for meaningful discussion of political philosophy. Even here, though, I deny the utility of asking thinkers like Hegel or Kant for guidance. German philosophy is notoriously a learned gibberish. For nearly two centuries, it has been used to justify every imaginable lapse from humanity and common sense. Dr Kruger is supposed to be an expert on Edmund Burke. It is worth asking why he has, on this occasion, avoided all attempt at imitating the clear English of the Enlightenment.

The likeliest answer is that enlightenment is not among his intentions. As said, that must be to express himself in a manner that almost none of his readers will understand. This book has been sent out for review to hundreds of journalists and general formers of opinion. It is hoped that these will all skim though it and scratch their heads. "What a bright young man this is" we are all to say. "What he says is all above my head, but I do not wish to look stupid, so will join in the applause at his erudition and profundity."

It is all like the story of the Emperor's New Clothes. Newspaper articles will be written about the "intellectual revival" in the Conservative Party. Gossip columns will be filled with references to the gigantic intellect of Dr Kruger. Even hostile articles about Mr Cameron will contain some flattering mention of the philosophical depths with which he has been put in touch.

If this were all one could say about his book, there would be much reason to condemn Dr Kruger. But there is more. His book is not only pretentious and obscure. It is also incompetent. If he were one of my students, and he were to offer this to me as a long undergraduate essay, he would have it thrown straight back in his face.

Look at this:

> But the 1980s also saw the defoliation of the natural landscape. In *The City of God* Augustine quotes a Briton saying 'the Romans make a desert and they call it peace'.[p.2]

Never mind that defoliation happens to trees, not natural landscapes. What matters here is that St Augustine did not say this, and could not have said it, bearing in mind the purpose of his *City of God*. The correct reference is to Tacitus in his biography of Agricola: "*Auferre, trucidare, rapere, falsis nominibus imperium atque ubi solitudinem faciunt pacem appellant*". Dr Kruger went, I believe, to an expensive public school, I to a comprehensive school in South London. Perhaps the classical languages are not so well studied in these former places as they once were. But anyone who wants to quote the ancients should make at least some effort to do it properly.

Is this pedantry? I do not think so. The quotation should be familiar to everyone of moderate education—even to people who do not know Latin. Its use is not absolutely required for the meaning of what Dr Kruger is trying to say. Like much else, it is there to impress. And he gets it wrong. And the fault is not confined to him. This book has gone through many drafts. Remember that it has been read and discussed by every intellectual close to the Conservative leadership. Even so, this glaring error on the second page was not picked up and corrected. This says more about the intellectual quality of modern Conservatives than anything else in the book.

Or take the casual reference on p.71 to Frédéric Bastiat as a "nineteenth-century anarchist". Bastiat believed in far less government than Dr Kruger or his employers. But he was a liberal, not an anarchist.

Or take this:

> Not everything that 'is permitted', said St Paul: 'is beneficial'.[p.55]

This is a reference to *1 Corinthians* 10:23: "All things are lawful for me, but all things are not expedient: all things are lawful for me, but all things edify not". The meaning of the verse is difficult, and may refer to the eating of sacrificial meat. It does nothing to advance whatever point Dr Kruger is making. It is, again, there to give an impression of learning that he does not seem, on examination, to possess.

Or take this:

> 'The state is an association' says Aristotle in the first sentence of *The Politics*.[p.79]

Aristotle may not have said this. In Greek, he says—and do pardon the Roman transliteration—"*epeide pasan polin horomen koinosian...*". The word in question is given in the standard translations as "community". It might bear the Oakeshottian sense of "association"—but this is a gloss that needs to be explained.

Or—to inhale yet another blast of Teutonic hot air—take this:

> Hegel famously argued that the slave could be more 'free' than the master, for the slave is contextualised, subject to circumstances, and *related* to his fellows even if only through their common bondage. Even though he lacks liberty, one of the three rights of negative freedom (even slaves, in ancient Rome, had the right to life and property), he has more positive freedom than his master, whose wealth makes him independent, and so unrelated to others. The slave is *realised*, and the master is not.[p.70]

Regardless of whether Hegel actually said anything so ridiculous—not that I would put anything past him—these words astonish me. In the first place, Roman slaves did not have a right to life: they had, from fairly late in the Imperial period, a right not to be butchered by their masters without what a court run by other slaveholders considered to be good reason. Their property was at best a *peculium,* to which they had no legal right. In the second place, no playing with words can possibly obliterate the factual difference between freeman and slave. If Dr Kruger doubts this, I only wish I could oblige by chaining him to an oar for a few days, or putting him in one of those disgusting underground prisons, or setting him to tend the fish for Vedius Pollio.

Much else in this book is worth despising. These three sentences simply make me angry.

But I turn back to the foreign words. I have found three uses of *"Aufhebung"*. These all look like the products of a cut and paste operation. They are all unexplained. When I come across phrases like "the crash of Platonic speculation into Aristotelian reality"[p.19], I now find it worth asking if Dr Kruger himself has the foggiest idea what he is trying to say.

Some decent endnotes might help to answer this question. But the notes are about as slipshod as they could be without not being added at all. Quotations are referenced with the author and title and date of the relevant work. But no editions or page numbers are given. Bearing in mind the length and complexity of the works cited—by Adam Smith, Hegel and Hayek, for instance—we can legitimately wonder how many of these Dr Kruger has actually read.

Of course, I blame the Conservative leadership for trying to make us believe it intends to do other than continue the work of turning England into the sort of despotism that would have made James II gasp and stare. But I also blame Dr Kruger for executing his commission so incompetently. And I must blame many of my friends for having let their names be used as an endorsement of his efforts—and for having brought themselves into disrepute by not objecting to so many scandalous blunders.

Above all, I blame Civitas—otherwise the most authoritative and radical of modern policy institutes. It has published the longest petition of intellectual bankruptcy I have read in years. I do most strongly urge David Green to withdraw this book at once and remove it from the Civitas catalogue.

APPENDIX TWO: THE FUTILITY OF REGULATION

During the ten years to the 21st February 2007, the phrase "completely unregulated" occurs 153 times in the British newspaper press. In all cases, unless used satirically, the phrase is part of a condemnation of some activity. We are told that the advertising of food to children,[84] residential lettings agents,[85] funeral directors,[86] rock climbing,[87] alleged communication with the dead,[88] salons and tanning shops,[89] contracts for extended warranties on home appliances,[90] and anything to do with the Internet—that these are all "almost completely unregulated" or just "completely unregulated", and that the authorities had better do something about the fact.

This is, for the most part, ruling class propaganda. There are jobs in regulation. It is a means of intimidating potential opponents without resort to the more obvious oppressions of the criminal law. It is a means of imposing on ordinary people the lie that they are incompetent to decide matters for themselves, but need a class of guardians above them to see that they are not cheated or poisoned.

We can see this clearly expressed in the writings of Douglas Jay, a Minister in the Attlee Government of the 1940s:

> [I]n the case of nutrition and health, just as in the case of education, the gentleman in Whitehall really does know better what is good for the people than the people know themselves.[91]

But even supposing there were no definite ruling class agenda in these claims, regulation is still to be rejected on the grounds that it does not and cannot work in the interests of those whom it is intended to protect.

---

[84] Maxine Frith, "With one in four children overweight, the experts explain what can be done about it", *The Independent*, London, 26th May 2004.

[85] Miles Bagnall, "Just don't let them get away with it", *The Guardian*, Manchester and London, 15th May 2004.

[86] Cara Page, "Shocking cost of dying", *The Daily Record*, Glasgow, 11th May 2004.

[87] Ian Parri, "Feedback", *The Daily Post*, Liverpool, 31st December 2003.

[88] Nick Curtis, "and if you want to find a psychic", *The Evening Standard*, London, 12th September 2003.

[89] "Will You Sleep Well After Sessions On Sunbeds?", *The Bath Chronicle*, Bristol, 14th April 2003.

[90] Teresa Hunter, "Travel agents and electrical retailers ordered to play fair", *The Sunday Herald*, Edinburgh, 27th October 2002.

[91] Douglas Jay, *The Socialist Case*, London, Victor Gollancz, 1947, p. 258. Worth stressing here is that this was not some casual remark pounced on by a journalist and quoted out of context. It comes from the second revised edition of a book first published ten years previously, and is therefore the product of some consideration.

Case Study: The Pharmaceutical Industry

Let us take as an example regulation of the pharmaceutical industry. The big companies that dominate this industry are greedy, secretive and indifferent to the wishes or even needs of patients. They are often unable even to create products that work effectively and safely. The answer, almost everyone agrees, is tighter regulation of the market.

In its submission of August 2004 to the Commons Health Select Committee, the Consumers' Association argued that

> The Medicines and Healthcare products Regulatory Agency (MHRA) needs to ensure that all its work is undertaken in the interests of public health protection....
>
> Responsibility for monitoring all forms of pharmaceutical industry advertising and other promotion should be transferred to a new, independent advertising and information regulator. This regulator should adopt and proactively implement robust and transparent procedures to prevent misleading promotional campaigns—including all forms of covert promotion—as far as possible at the outset, and to take swift and effective action when these do occur. These procedures should be drawn up in consultation with all relevant parties, in particular, those representing the interests of patients, consumers and public health. Most importantly, they should maintain a clear focus on protecting public health and delivering public benefit.[92]

Yet is regulation the answer? The assumption behind much of what was presented to or discussed in these parliamentary hearings appears to have been that whatever wrong or merely questionable was done by the pharmaceutical companies could have been avoided by a better scheme of regulation, and that, the problems uncovered, the best use of intellectual effort must now be in devising a better scheme for the future. But what went wrong with the regulations already in place?

The answer is that the present regulatory body for the pharmaceutical industry—the Medicines and Healthcare Products Regulatory Agency (MHRA)—seems to have been too close to the industry for effective regulation to have taken place. In October 2004, *The Guardian* newspaper obtained documents that showed the nature of the relationship. Since 1989, when the then prime minister, Margaret Thatcher, took drug regulation out of the hands of the Department of Health, the MHRA has been wholly funded

---

[92] *Health Select Committee Inquiry into The Influence of the Pharmaceutical Industry: health policy, research, prescribing practice and patient use—August 2004 Memorandum from Consumers' Association*, para. 1.5—available on-line at:
  http://www.which.net/campaigns/health/medicines/0408pharma_scomm.pdf (checked June 2007)

by the pharmaceutical companies. Since then:

- The regulator and the industry have been engaged in a joint lobbying campaign in Europe;

- The industry privately drew up its own detailed blueprint of how the MHRA should be run;

- The industry has been pushing for higher level representation at the MHRA against ministers' wishes.[93]

John Abraham, professor of sociology at Sussex University, who is mainly known for his books on drug regulation, says that the MHRA has come to believe the interests of public health are coherent with the promotion of the industry. He says:

> The criticism of the old Department of Health medicines department in the 70s was that it didn't have any teeth. Not only does it now not have any teeth, but it is not motivated to bite.[94]

He further claims that there is too much of the "revolving door" syndrome at the MHRA. Not only does it take fees from the pharmaceutical industry, but many agency officials used to work for pharmaceutical companies, such as the former head of worldwide drug safety at GlaxoSmithKline, who is now the MHRA's head of licensing. It was with these facts in mind that the Consumers' Association has called for a new regulatory body.

However, what appears to have happened with pharmaceutical regulation is not some aberration that can be improved with a new legal framework. It is no more than the illustration of a general tendency.

Market Failure as an Argument

The justification for a regulatory body where pharmaceutical products are concerned is what economists call "market failure". The mainstream defence of the free market rests on the claim that it allocates resources more efficiently than any other system. To speak formally, it tends to bring about both productive and allocative efficiency. This first means that goods and services are produced at the lowest currently known cost. The second means that production satisfies the known wants of consumers in the fullest way currently possible.

We can best see this argument in the analysis of firms under perfect competition. Let it be granted that there are many buyers and sellers in a

---

[93] Rob Evans and Sarah Boseley, "The drugs industry and its watchdog: a relationship too close for comfort?", *The Guardian*, London and Manchester, 4th October 2004.
[94] *Ibid.*

market; that all the goods produced in this market are of the same quality; that there are no barriers to entry or exit for any player in the market; that there is perfect knowledge among all players in the market regarding prices and production methods. Given these assumptions, an equilibrium between demand and supply will come about that maximises social welfare. Any intervention by the authorities in such a state of affairs will produce a loss of welfare.

Now, such an equilibrium never comes about in the real world. It certainly never comes about in the pharmaceutical product market. There are not large numbers of buyers and sellers, nor are goods of the same quality—instead, there is a group of very large companies with virtual monopolies in certain products, facing a virtually monopsonistic buyer in each national market: in Britain, this is the National Health Service. There are obvious barriers to entry and exit.

Above all, there is not perfect knowledge. There is instead what is called the problem of asymmetric information. The pharmaceutical companies know all that can be humanly known about their products: the consuming public knows almost nothing, and is not thought able to learn what needs to be known.

Regulation as the Answer

This being so, the overwhelming consensus of opinion is that some regulatory body is needed to stand between the pharmaceutical companies and the consuming public. The functions of this body are to ask the appropriate questions, and only to allow products to be sold if the answers are satisfactory. Given sufficient zeal by or trust in the regulatory body, there is no need for the public to ask its own questions. Indeed, there is a case for the public not to be allowed to find out information for itself. The public may be too ill-informed about the nature of what is being discussed to understand the nature and quality of the information provided—especially as much information will come from sources that are themselves ill-informed. Therefore, in the United Kingdom, the Medicines and Healthcare Products Regulatory Agency also bans on the advertising of pharmaceutical products, and a very tight control over what information can be released to the public.

The Politics of Regulatory Capture

The main problem with this approach, however, is not incidental but systemic. It is what pubic choice economists call "regulatory capture".

The phrase comes from Gabriel Kolko, a Marxist historian, who made his name with research into the Progressive Era in America[95] and into American

---

[95] Gabriel Kolko, *The Triumph of Conservatism: A Reinterpretation of American History, 1900-*

railway regulation. [96] He applied the phrase to a specific phenomenon: when regulators serve the interests of those they are allegedly regulating in the general public interest. It was known before Professor Kolko's work, but regarded as an aberration. Professor Kolko examined the growth of American federal regulation in the early 20th century, and argued that regulatory capture was not just common, but in fact the norm. He found no important exception to its emerging, and usually emerging very early, in the history of a regulatory agency.

Professor Kolko argued that whatever liberal reformers might have intended, and whatever the public may have believed, business interests took control of the actual regulatory process early on and made it work for them.

The basic mechanics of regulatory capture are straightforward. People give more attention to a particular law or agency if they feel that they have something at stake. They will make sure to know about laws and policies that affect their own interests. If those people are running a wealthy business, they will have a lot at stake, and will correspondingly make sure to be fully informed.

Now, regulators may at first feel hostile to their subjects. Over time, however, regulators and the regulated get to know each other and to work together, with or without any real sense of cooperation. The regulated, who provide information and make a show of cooperation, earn the appreciation of regulators, who find that endless crusade takes its toll in energy, enthusiasm, and efficiency. Regulators find that if they cooperate with their subjects in some areas, they will get cooperation back on others.

In addition, those of the regulated who gain the sympathy of regulators as "team players", "responsible, cooperative enterprises", and the like get favours. The problem is that incremental small shifts can add up to big consequences. Over years and decades, the net effect of such shifts in the course of regulation is to draw the regulatory agency in directions that the public is likely neither to understand nor to feel represents the original intent of the legislation that created the agency.

There is no need for regulators and regulated to like each other. Often they do not. They still work together. Regulators hardly ever want to destroy what they regulate. Most often, they see their job as simply a matter of imposing the public interest on otherwise irresponsible organisations. And the regulated usually regard the regulators as facts of life to deal with, and better cooperated

---

1916, The Free Press, New York, 1963—selections available on-line at:
 http://users.crocker.com/~acacia/kolko.html (checked June 2007)
[96] Gabriel Kolko, *Railroads and Regulation, 1877-1916*, Princeton University Press, Princeton, N.J.1965

with than resisted outright.

Regulated firms end up supplying not just data to regulators, but personnel. After all, who understands the field better than folks who are retiring or resigning from the field's major participants? Few people want regulations made in outright ignorance. The result is a regulatory agency staffed by former or perhaps future colleagues of those in the regulated firms.

Every so often, incidental details of this process will come to light. See, for example, *The Guardian* report cited above. Sometimes, the details will verge on the scandalous—see, for example, the revelations of the late 1990s about the body set up to regulate the British National Lottery. But the overwhelming evidence is that it is impossible to ensure that the regulators and regulated in any scheme of regulation will not eventually come to regard each other in at least many important respects as allies, and to ensure that regulation works in what objective third parties might regard as the public interest.

The answer to these alleged problems of market failure is to attack the institutional foundations that allow big companies to exist, and then to leave ordinary people to choose for themselves, assisted by the civil law of contract and of torts, and by private institutions like the Consumers' Association.

INDEX

Other Books by Sean Gabb

The Column of Phocas: A Novel of Murder and Intrigue Set in Mediæval Rome, 2006, 256pp ISBN: 0 9541032 4 6, £8.99/$20

Smoking, Class and the Legitimation of Power, 2005, 196pp, ISBN: 0 9541032 0 3, £18.99/$40

War and the National Interest: Arguments for a British Foreign Policy, 2005, 125pp, ISBN: 0 9541032 3 8, £18.99/$40

Dispatches from a Dying Country: Reflections on Modern England, Introduction by Chris R. Tame, 2001, 234pp, ISBN: 0 9541032 0 3, £20/$40

Available from

The Hampden Press
Suite 35, 2 Landsdowne Row
London W1J 6HL
England

A Word about Money

Have you enjoyed reading this book? Has it in any sense enlightened and inspired you? Would you like to see more of the same? If yes, why not send Sean Gabb some money? This will allow him to print more copies of this book and distribute them free to opinion formers, to students and to other persons who might find it interesting or useful, and so that he can give proper attention to writing the next.

If you really want to encourage him to write more, you should consider giving Dr Gabb some money!

Please make all cheques (£/US$/€) payable to "The Hampden Press" and send to the Hampden Press at the address given above.

Or you can donate on-line with your credit card or *via* PayPal by going here: **http://tinyurl.com/34e2o3**

Dr Gabb can be reached at *sean@libertarian.co.uk*